BIG
ENGLISH ⑤
PLUS

T0385973

Mario Herrera • Christopher Sol Cruz

PUPIL'S BOOK

Contents

CLIL/Culture	Writing	Life Skills/Project	Phonics	I can...
Science: The two sides of the brain analyse, determine, exchange, hemisphere, personality, practical, take care of **Additional language:** Compound adjectives **Around the World: Early Olympic events** competition, event, motor vehicle, race course, sporting, variation	News article	**Be a team player.** Talk about working together. Make a poster to find new members of a team, club or group.	**ce, ci, cir** cell, centre cinema, city circle, circus	...make suggestions. ...talk about my interests. ...talk about the present and the past.
Science: Animal mothers behaviour, give birth, jaws, mammal, maternal instinct, offspring, powerful, sight **Additional language:** Quantity: *some, many, all* **Around the World: Traditions around the world** into, respectively, ribbon, sneak, stuff, symbolise, tradition, treat	Autobiography	**Keep family traditions.** Talk about family traditions. Make a class book about family traditions.	**ge, gi, gy** gel, gem ginger, giraffe gym, gypsy	...talk about important life events and habits of the past. ...make comparisons.
Art: Effective posters or advertisements bold, effective, focus, get across, image, impatient, invisible, layout **Additional language:** Zero conditionals with *if* **Around the World: Helping others** animal shelter, benefit, cancer, cause, donate, fortune, proof, raise, rescue, supplies, tutoring, volunteer	Letter	**Help others.** Talk about international charities. Write a fundraising plan and create an advert for an event.	**lk, mb** chalk, talk, walk climb, comb, lamb	...talk about helping others and about fundraising activities. ...talk about possibilities and experiences. ...say what I'm going to do.
History: The history of money bartering, bronze, coin, currency, exchange, grain, livestock, seal, trade **Additional language:** Prepositions: *during, over, until* **Around the World: Shopping places** browse, experience, features, haggle, products, user's manual, vendor	Product review	**Develop good money habits.** Talk about what you do with your money. Design a shopping bag that encourages good spending habits.	**sc, ho** muscle, scene, science echo, ghost, honest	...talk about shopping. ...make comparisons.
Maths: Calculations addition, customer, item, multiplication, power cut, price list, receipt, serve, souvenir **Additional language:** *need to, needn't* **Around the World: Holiday destinations** arctic, expedition, fascinating, founder, frozen, guide, guided tour, head over, igloo, particularly, poison, poisonous	Postcards	**Be safe on holiday.** Talk about holidays and safety tips. Make a holiday safety poster.	**cl, tw** clap, clock, clown twelve, twist, twin	...talk about holiday problems. ...ask and answer about what was going on when something happened.
Science: How robots help us assistive, capabilities, complicated, gestures, procedures, repetitive, robotic, socially, special needs, surgical **Around the World: Endangered languages** communicate, dialect, dictionary, extinct, fluently, generation, healing, official, pass on, preserve	Diary entry	**Have dreams for the future.** Talk about future dreams. Design an advert for a product or service in the future.	**pp, bb, dd, mm, nn, tt** happy hobby ladder summer tennis butter	... ask questions and make predictions about the future. ...talk about technology.
Social Science: Important inventions candle, cash register, combustion engine, fuel, invention/inventor, organise, plumbing, pump, vehicle, well, wheel **Around the World: Cool transformations** combine, connect, dock, innovative, natural resource, speakers, supplier, transform	Description: Object	**Appreciate history.** Talk about your culture and learn the importance of appreciating history. Make a class book about items from different cultures.	**lt, lk, ld, lb** belt milk, silk cold, field bulb	...guess what things are or might be. ...say what things are used for or used to do. ...make true sentences using conditionals.
Science: How fresh produce travels country of origin, diesel, distribution centre, fresh produce, imported, local, locally-grown, petrol, pollution, seasonal, shipping, typical **Additional language:** Conjunction: *so* **Around the World: Where products came from** borders, chemical, county, engineer, explorer, fridge, novelty, power tools	Persuasive writing	**Appreciate what you eat and use every day.** Talk about things you appreciate and where they come from. Make a poster about things you appreciate and where they come from.	**lf, lp, lm** elf, golf help elm, film	...talk about where goods come from. ...talk about products and the materials used to make them. ...use the passive voice and defining relative clauses.
Science: The effects of adrenalin adrenal glands, adrenalin, air, cells, heart, hormone, lungs, oxygen, prehistoric, protect, release, stress **Around the World: Risky activities** aerialist, antenna, board, competitive diver, extreme sports, parachute, professional, risk, tightrope, trick, warrior	Description: Experience	**Explore your surroundings.** To learn the value of exploring your surroundings. Make a collage about things to explore in your community.	**ft, ct, mp, sk** left, raft fact camp, lamp risk	...talk about experiences. ...talk about preferences.

MY INTERESTS

4

1 Read about these famous people. What were they interested in? Complete the sentences with a word from the box. Then listen and check.

| computer | football | mathematics | money | music |

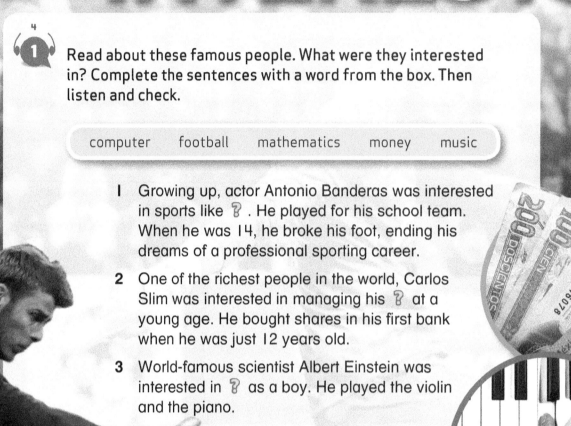

1 Growing up, actor Antonio Banderas was interested in sports like ❓ . He played for his school team. When he was 14, he broke his foot, ending his dreams of a professional sporting career.

2 One of the richest people in the world, Carlos Slim was interested in managing his ❓ at a young age. He bought shares in his first bank when he was just 12 years old.

3 World-famous scientist Albert Einstein was interested in ❓ as a boy. He played the violin and the piano.

4 Actress Emma Stone always wanted to act. She was also good at using a ❓ . When she was 14, she used a PowerPoint presentation to convince her parents to let her begin a career in acting.

5 As a young woman, architect and artist Maya Lin loved bird-watching, hiking and studying ❓ .

2 Match the names of the school groups to the pictures. Then listen and check.

basketball team	drama club	school newspaper
school orchestra	science club	tae kwon do club

1

2

3

4

5

6

3 Read. Look at 2. Which school group should each pupil join?

1 Dan loves jogging and playing sports. He's got a lot of free time.

2 Dina loves acting. Someday, she would like to star in a film.

3 Milan is good at writing and has got his own blog.

4 Paul likes martial arts and is very athletic. He likes playing chess, too.

5 Jane is interested in building robots. She's good at Science and Maths.

6 Sara likes playing the trumpet. She's good at it, too.

4 Work with a partner. Ask and answer.

What's Dan interested in doing?

Which school group should he join?

He's interested in jogging and playing sports.

The basketball team!

THINK BIG Which activities could you still do as an adult? Have adults got similar interests to young people? Why/Why not?

5 Listen and read. When are the football team try-outs?

| Home | School Library | Cafeteria Menu | For Parents |

The Grove School News

GET BUSY AFTER SCHOOL!

Welcome back to school! From all the staff here at your school news blog, we hope you're ready for another great year. Have you signed up for an after-school activity yet? If not, don't worry! There's still time. Here are some of the activities you can try:

Tony Underwood scoring the winning goal at last year's county championships

SPORTS TEAMS

Do you like sports? How about joining the football or athletics team? Both teams have try-outs next Monday and Tuesday at 3:00. Last year, our school football team won the county championships but many of our best players have moved up to secondary school. So now the team needs new players. For more information, contact our sports advisors, Ms Matte or Mr Stergis.

Sam Penny showing his artistic talents

GOOD AT ART?

This year, your classmates in the school art club plan to paint a mural on the wall by the office. So they need new members to help create it! Are you interested in drawing, painting or taking photographs? This club is for you. The first meeting of the school year is next Wednesday at 3:15 in room 221. Please see Ms Greenway for more information.

NEW THIS YEAR

There are some new activities you can have a go at. Try the new after-school science club! It has plans to enter the national Junior Robotics competition this year. So if you want to try building a robot, this club is for you. See Mr Larson in room 105 for more details. The club meets every Thursday.

Do you like acting? Are you good at singing? The school play this year is a musical – *The Sound of Music*. Come and try out next Monday or Wednesday afternoon in the school auditorium. Sign-up sheets for auditions are on the wall outside room 125.

For a list of all the after-school activities this year, click here. Or pick up a membership form from the advisor's office – room 103.

Comments

dharrison
Don't forget the karate club! We need members, too! Anyone interested in joining should contact Mr Silver.

agrell
Robots? Cool! Count me in!

apritchett
Acting in the school play was so much fun last year. And I love singing. I want to try out again!

READING COMPREHENSION

6 Answer the questions with a partner.

1 Which school team won a big competition last year?

2 Where can you get more information about the science club?

3 When are the auditions for the school play?

4 What's the art club planning to do this year?

5 Where can you find a complete list of all the after-school activities?

 THINK BIG Which activities in the article interest you? Why?
Are you interested in doing any of your school's activities or joining any clubs? Why/Why not?

7 Listen and read. What's Henry good at? Practise the dialogue with a partner.

Ms Parks:	Henry, I was wondering. Are you interested in joining a club this year?
Henry:	I am but I'm not sure which one to join.
Ms Parks:	How about joining the science club? You're good at building things.
Henry:	Maybe… When do they meet?
Ms Parks:	Every Monday after school.
Henry:	Oh, I can't. I've got guitar lessons on Mondays.
Ms Parks:	OK. Well, how about joining the art club?
Henry:	The art club?
Ms Parks:	Yes. You're so good at drawing. And they meet on Tuesdays.
Henry:	Tuesdays are fine for me. I think I'll do it.

8 Practise the dialogue in 7 with a partner.

9 Listen and match the after-school activities to the timetables. Then say what each pupil is interested in.

acting   playing football   reading comics   writing   busy = ■

1 M T W Th F   2 M T W Th F   3 M T W Th F   4 M T W Th F

a    b    c    d

| How about **joining** the drama club? | No, thanks. I'm not good at **acting**. |
| How about **trying out** for the basketball team? | OK. I love **playing** basketball. |

Tip: Use the gerund form of the verb (verb + *ing*) after *How about, love, like, enjoy, be interested in* and *be good at*.

10 Use the words to help you make questions.

1 football team/try out

2 school newspaper/join

3 school musical/try out

4 English club/join

5 school orchestra/try out

6 hiking club/join

11 Complete the sentences with the correct form of the verb in brackets.

1 No, thanks. I'm not very good at ❓. (sing)

2 Sounds great. I'm really interested in ❓ more English. (learn)

3 Good idea. I love ❓ the violin. (play)

4 Why not? I like ❓ football a lot. (play)

5 Oh, no! I don't enjoy ❓ at all. (walk)

6 I don't think so. I'm not interested in ❓ articles. (write)

12 Match the questions and answers in 10 and 11. Practise the dialogues with a partner. Then take turns asking and answering the questions again with your own answers.

How about trying out for the football team?

I don't think so. I'm...

13 What are your favourite hobbies and activities? Do they have to do more with logic and memory or imagination and creativity? Discuss with a partner.

14 Listen and read. Which side of your brain might be stronger if you're good at remembering people's names?

> **CONTENT WORDS**
> analyse   determine   exchange   hemisphere
> personality   practical   take care of

Left Brained or Right Brained?

Did you know that what you're good at doing might have something to do with the side of your brain you use most? You see, the brain is divided into two hemispheres (sides) – the left hemisphere and the right hemisphere. Each hemisphere takes care of different things but the two exchange information between them. Some scientists believe that each side of the brain controls different abilities and that each person has one side that's stronger. That stronger side may help determine, in some ways, what we like to do, what we're good at and what we're interested in.

Left-brained people are logical. They're good at analysing details. They enjoy doing things like solving Maths problems and playing chess. Right-brained people are creative and imaginative. They're good at activities like painting and acting. But there are also scientists who say that although there may be some truth to this theory, things aren't so simple. They add that the brain works in a very complicated way and we don't know everything about it yet.

Which side of your brain is stronger?

If you would like to find out which side of your brain is stronger, take this short quiz. Choose (A) or (B) to answer each question.

1 Do you prefer going to (A) Maths lessons or (B) Art lessons?

2 Do you like (A) planning everything or (B) not planning at all?

3 Do you like (A) lots of instructions or (B) not many instructions?

4 Do you remember things more easily (A) with words or (B) with pictures?

5 When you meet people, do you remember (A) their name or (B) their face?

6 When you read a story, do you look for (A) details or (B) the big picture?

How did you score? If you got more As, the left side of your brain may be stronger. If you got more Bs, the right side is probably stronger. Now think about the kinds of activities you like to do. Do they match your brain type?

THINK BIG What do you think of your test score? Is it accurate? Do you think people can be clearly divided like this?

15 Look at 14. Choose the correct word(s).

1 There's **some/no** communication between the two sides of our brain.

2 Most people use one side of their brain **only/more than the other**.

3 **Both sides/The stronger side** of the brain is connected with what we're good at.

4 **Left/Right** –brained people are good at the arts.

5 Some scientists believe that this theory **may be/is definitely** wrong.

16 Work with a partner. Which side of the brain is connected with being very good at doing these things? Say left or right.

1 Remembering people's names.

2 Remembering people's faces.

3 Telling or writing stories.

4 Following complicated instructions.

5 Learning by watching someone do something instead of reading how to do it.

6 Planning and doing things in an organised way.

17 Look at 16. Find out if your partner is left or right brained. Ask and answer.

Are you good at remembering people's names?

Oh, no. I'm awful at remembering names!

18 Think about your partner's answers in 17. Do the results from your discussion match the results of the test in 14? Write about your partner's profile in your notebook.

Sam is more right-brained than left-brained. He isn't good at

remembering names or instructions. He enjoys painting and being creative.

He doesn' t like planning things in detail.

19 Look, listen and read. What language is Cassie learning?

Leyla and Cassie are talking on the phone.

Leyla: Jess and I are leaving for the cinema now. Are you coming?

Cassie: I can't. I'm doing my Chinese homework.

Leyla: But you don't speak Chinese. And you never do homework on a Friday evening.

Cassie: Well, I'm learning Chinese now. I started yesterday.

Leyla: Why?

Cassie: Because we just got a Shih Tzu puppy. His name's Pookie. Shih Tzu dogs come from China. How will Pookie know what I'm saying if I don't speak his language?

Leyla: You *are* kidding, aren't you?

 20 Read and complete.

Present Simple

+	Shih Tzu dogs **come** from China. Pookie ¹ from China.
-	You **don't speak** Chinese. Pookie ² **speak** English.
?	³ they **go** to the cinema every weekend? **Does** Jose ⁴ any other language?

Present Continuous

+	I'm ⁵ my Chinese homework. They ⁶ **talking** on the phone.
-	We **aren't doing** anything tonight. Elisa ⁷ **staying** in tonight.
?	⁸ you kidding me? **Is** Brit **going** out tonight?

Past Simple

+	I **started** yesterday. They **got** the dog from a kennel.
-	He **didn't come** all the way from China. Cassie and Jess ⁹ **know** about the dog.
?	¹⁰ you **find** the dialogue funny? **Did** Brian **mean** what he said?

21 Complete the sentences.

1 ❓ (Ahmad/not play) sports. ❓ (he/run) 5 kilometres every morning, though.

2 ❓ (you/play) the guitar very well. How often ❓ (you/practise)?

3 ❓ (we/have) to get up at 6 a.m. on weekdays, so ❓ (we/not get up) early on Saturdays.

4 ❓ (they/live) near the beach. ❓ (they/go) swimming in winter?

5 ❓ (I/not think) she's going to come with us. ❓ (she/not like) hiking.

6 ❓ (the shirt/fit) quite well but ❓ (the colour/be) good?

22 Who's doing what? Ask and answer.

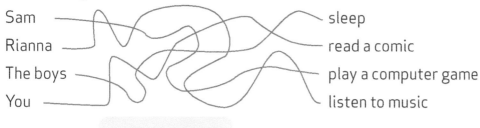

Sam
Rianna
The boys
You

sleep
read a comic
play a computer game
listen to music

Is Sam sleeping?

No, he isn't. He's playing a computer game.

23 Read Cassie's list of things she had to do last weekend. Write what she did and what she didn't do.

- give Pookie a bath ✔
- buy dog food ✔
- take Pookie for a walk ✘
- visit grandma ✘
- watch the music awards on TV ✔
- finish school project ✘

1 She gave Pookie a bath.

24 Work with a partner. Ask and answer for you.

1 What do you usually do at the weekend? Did you do anything different last weekend?

2 What after-school activities do you do? When did you start?

3 Where did you go on your last holiday? Did you enjoy it?

4 What type of films do you like watching? Which was the last film you watched? What was it about?

You'd Never Guess These Were Olympic Sports!

One of the world's most popular sporting events, the Olympics, is older than you might think. It started almost 3,000 years ago, around 776 BC, in ancient Greece. [1] ?

Some of the early Modern Olympic events are the same ones we see today. [2] ? But some of them came and went so fast that few people remember that they were once part of the Olympic Games. Let's take a look back at those events that were just too strange or not popular enough to stay.

1 Skijoring

The name *skijoring* means 'ski-driving' in Norwegian. In this sport, a horse pulls a person on skis over a race course covered in snow. It actually looks a lot like water skiing! This strange sport from Norway was part of the Winter Olympics only once, in 1928. [3] ? Dogs or a motor vehicle instead of a horse pull the skier in variations of this sport.

2 Hot Air Ballooning

During the Paris Olympics of 1900, hot air ballooning was introduced to the Olympic Games. Players competed to see how far and high they could go or how long they could stay in the air. [4] ?

25 What's your favourite Olympic event? Discuss in groups.

16
26 Listen and read. Which of the events in paragraphs 1–4 were part of the 1900 Olympics?

> **CONTENT WORDS**
> competition   event   motor vehicle   race course   sporting   variation

27 Look at 26 and put the sentences in the correct place.
  a   You could say that for the British teams winning was 'child's play'!
  b   The first Modern Olympics were held in Athens in 1896.
  c   It's still played in countries where there's lots of snow in winter.
  d   They also had to land as close as possible to a spot marked on the ground.
  e   Other events were added in later years.
  f   The other player was from Belgium.

3 Tug-of-War

Did you know that in 1900, 1904, 1908, 1912 and 1920, tug-of-war, a popular game with children all over the world, was a regular Olympic event? The Olympic tug-of-war competition had eight players at each end of a long rope. The team that pulled the other team 2 metres won the event. In the five years of this Olympic game, Great Britain won the most medals in this event. [5]

4 Croquet

The only time croquet was an Olympic event was in the 1900 Paris Olympics. France won all the events but this was no surprise as 9 out of the 10 players were French! [6]

To be fair, some of the events that are still part of the Olympics don't look less weird than the ones we mentioned above. Can you think of any?

---

28 Make a Sport Fact Card about a sport you like doing or watching or about an unusual sport. Then present it to the class.

Rugby	
Where?	Outdoors on a rugby field
Who?	Two teams of fifteen players
What?	Rugby ball, two rugby posts
How?	Each team scores by touching the ball over a line and by kicking the ball between the posts.
Olympic Game?	Not yet

Rugby is an outdoor sport. It's a team sport. There are fifteen players on each team. It's played on a rugby field. Players need a rugby ball and two rugby posts. Each team has to score by touching the ball down over a line and by kicking the ball between the posts. It isn't an Olympic sport.

29 Read the article. Then study the questions and answers below.

> **The Grove School News**
>
> Our school science club went to the national Junior Robotics
> Competition last month. The competition took place at the
> Science Museum in London. The science club won fifth place.
> We're very proud of our science club! All of the students in it are
> good at designing and building robots. We're sure they'll be happy
> to show you the award-winning robots. Just ask any member of
> the science club.

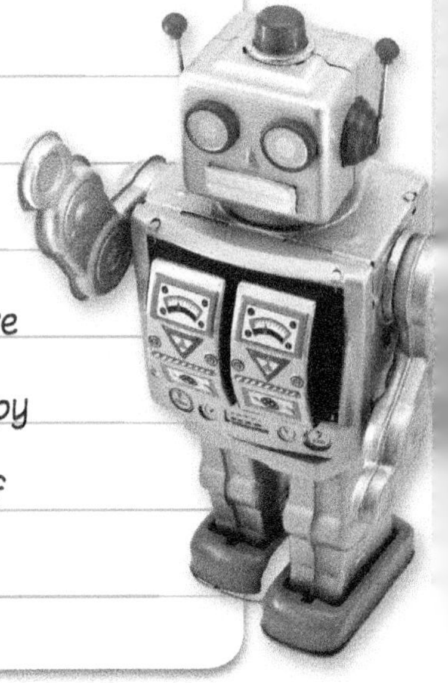

When?	What happened?
1 Who?	school science club
2 What?	national Junior Robotics Competition
3 Where?	Science Museum, London
4 When?	last month
5 What happened?	they won fifth place

30 Prepare a news article about a club, team or group at your school. Copy the chart above into your notebook and answer the questions to help you gather information.

31 Display your articles on a school noticeboard or use them to put together a school newspaper of your own.

THINK BIG Apart from a school newspaper, what else could you write articles for?

32 Which person in each picture is not being a team player? How can that person become a team player? Discuss with a partner.

1

2

3

He needs to pass the ball!

I agree.

33 Are you a team player? Discuss with a partner. When do you need to work in a team? Give three examples.

PROJECT

34 Make a poster to find new members for a club, team or group at your school.

Join the Art Club

Are you good at drawing?
Do you like doing art projects?

How about joining the art club?

The club meets every Tuesday after school.

35 Listen, read and repeat.

1 c-e ce   **2** c-i ci   **3** c-ir cir

 36 Listen and blend the sounds.

1 c-e-ll	cell	**2** c-i-t-y	city
3 c-ir-c-u-s	circus	**4** c-i-n-e-m-a	cinema
5 c-e-n-tre	centre	**6** c-ir-c-le	circle

 37 Listen and chant.

Have fun in the city!
Go to the cinema.
Have fun in the city!
Go to the centre.

 38 Work with a partner. Read the directions, listen to the model and play.

1 Partner A numbers the School Club or Group Cards from 1–6 in any order in their notebook. Partner B numbers the Interest Cards from 1–6 in any order.

2 Partner A makes a suggestion and Partner B answers, using an Interest Card with the same number.

3 If Partner B's interests don't match Partner A's suggestion, Partner A offers another suggestion. Partners cross out each card in their notebook as it is used.

School Club or Group Cards

chess club   school orchestra   drama club   school newspaper   football team   tae kwon do club

Interest Cards

sing   play board games   do martial arts   play the trumpet   play sports   write

39 Match the activities to the correct groups.

1 school newspaper

2 school orchestra

3 tae kwon do club

4 art club

5 science club

a building robots

b writing articles

c drawing

d playing a musical instrument

e painting

f taking photos

g doing martial arts

40 Complete the dialogue with words from the box. Use the correct verb form.

> do   join   like   not take up   practise   sign up   try out   write

John: What do you do after school? Are you in any school clubs this year?

Sally: No, but I'm thinking about ¹ for one.

John: Well, how about the gymnastics club? You ² gymnastics last year, didn't you?

Sally: That's true but I haven't got time for that club. They ³ five days a week.

John: How about ⁴ for the basketball team?

Sally: I'm not really interested in ⁵ sports right now.

John: Really? Well, I can see that you ⁶ an article on your laptop right now.

Sally: Yes, I am.

John: Then how about ⁷ the school news bloggers? They always need people. And blogging ⁸ that much time!

Sally: Hmm… good idea. I might just do that.

I Can

• make suggestions.   • talk about my interests.   • talk about the present and the past.

unit 2 FAMILY TIES

22
1 Read and answer the questions about families. Then listen and check.

1 **How Many Mackenzies?**

Mr and Mrs Mackenzie have six daughters and each daughter has one brother. How many people are in the Mackenzie family?

2 **Family Name Trivia**

What's the most common family name in the world: Chang, García or Smith?

3 **Big Families**

Which country has got the largest average household size: Italy, Canada or Colombia?

4 **Good Grief, Grandma!**

Bai Ulan Kudanding, a woman in the southern Philippines, has 14 children, 107 grandchildren, 138 great-grandchildren and two great-great-grandchildren. She knows all of their names! How many children are there in all?

2 Listen and find the family members in the photos. Use words from the box to name them.

Calderon Family

| me | my aunt and uncle | my baby sister |
| my dad | my mum | my older brother |

1

2

3

4

 3 Copy the chart into your notebook. Listen again and complete the chart.

What?	Who?	Where?	When?
1 moved	Andrea, her older brother Pedro and their mum and dad	Brighton	2012
2 opened a restaurant			
3 was born			
4 got married		~	~
5 graduated from cooking school			

4 Work with a partner. Ask and answer about the Calderon family.

When was her baby sister born?

She was born in 2012.

THINK BIG What challenges can you think of for a family moving to a new country?

Listen and read. How many Flying Maliceks are there now?

The Biggest Circus Family
IN THE WORLD
by Zach Malicek

My name's Zach and I'm from a big family. I mean, it's a *really* big family. My last name is Malicek. Maybe you don't know us but we're the biggest circus family in the world. We're 'The Flying Maliceks'! We weren't always the biggest circus act, though. When my Grandpa Viktor started as a trapeze performer in Slovakia, there was only one Flying Malicek: him!

My grandpa moved to the United Kingdom when he was about 20 years old. He quickly found a circus job working in his new country. A few years later, Grandpa Viktor married my Grandma Irina. Grandpa taught my grandma how to perform on the trapeze and soon there were two Flying Maliceks. My grandma didn't perform all the time, though. She took time off to have a few babies. She had eight of them, actually!

My father Daniel is the youngest child in the family. He has five brothers and two sisters – my uncles and aunts. And all of them learnt to perform on the trapeze when they were children. The people at the circus love watching the Flying Maliceks. And we all love watching their excited faces when we fly through the air.

My grandpa and grandma are getting older now. They retired from performing about five years ago. But the Flying Maliceks aren't getting smaller – we're getting bigger! I have two older sisters and we all perform in the act. My aunts and uncles all have children; and they perform, too. In total there are 37 of us! Can you believe it?

Last year, we were on TV. We had our own reality show called *Circus Family*. Some people from the TV show followed

us around with cameras all the time. It was exciting but sometimes I wanted them to go away! One special thing happened when we were on that show. My cousin Gillian met a cameraman and six months ago they got married. Now he's learning the trapeze, too!

READING COMPREHENSION

6 Complete the sentences with the correct numbers.

1 Viktor moved to the United Kingdom when he was ? years old.

2 Zach's father is the youngest of ? children.

3 Zach has got ? uncles and ? aunts.

4 Zach has got ? older sisters.

5 Gillian got married ? months ago.

THINK BIG Why do you think the Flying Maliceks are getting bigger?
How many people are there in a 'big' family?
What are the good things about being part of a big family?

Language in Action

7 Listen and read. What does Darren learn about Amelia?

Darren: Who's that?

Amelia: Oh, that's my older brother Armando. That was a long time ago. I think he was about 12 in that photo.

Darren: Oh, do you have an older brother?

Amelia: Yes. He's a lot older than I am. He's 25. He lives in London.

Darren: Really?

Amelia: Yes. He moved to London when he was 23. He works in a hotel.

Darren: That's nice. Mmm… you look like him… a little bit.

Amelia: Do you think so? Maybe. But he's really tall now. Actually, he's about six feet tall. He's the tallest person in our family.

8 Practise the dialogue in 7 with a partner.

9 Listen and match. Then say. Use the correct form of a verb from the box.

be born   get married   graduate   move

1 She 🔊   2 They 🔊   3 I 🔊   4 We 🔊

a   b   c   d

<table>
<tr><td>We went to Edinburgh <u>when</u> I was eight.
<u>When</u> they were children, they lived in Manchester.</td></tr>
<tr><td>She moved to Cambridge three years <u>ago</u>.
A few months <u>later</u>, she got a new job.</td></tr>
<tr><td>Tip: Look for signal words like when, later and ago.</td></tr>
</table>

Present simple	→	Past simple
go	→	went
am	→	was
are	→	were
live	→	lived
get	→	got
move	→	moved

10 **Complete the paragraph. Use the correct form of the verbs.**

This is my older sister Lisa. She's very happy today because, a few hours ago, she ¹ ⧠ (buy) her first car! She saved money from all her part-time jobs. She ² ⧠ (get) her first job a long time ago when she ³ ⧠ (be) only 11 years old. She delivered newspapers in our neighbourhood. Later, when she was 14, she ⁴ ⧠ (start) to tutor younger children after school. Then when Lisa was 16, she ⁵ ⧠ (find) a job at a restaurant. She ⁶ ⧠ (work) there almost every weekend when she was in the sixth form. Then, a week ago, she finally ⁷ ⧠ (have) enough money to buy a car.
I'm very proud of my sister. She works really hard!

> Sue's **taller than** Yoko and Mark.
>
> Sue's **the tallest** person in our class.

11 **Look at the pictures and make sentences.**

1
Mark   Isabelle   Claire

2
Spot   Fido   Blue

3
James   Sally   Robert

1 (short) ⧠ is the shortest.

2 (small) ⧠ is smaller than ⧠ .

3 (young) ⧠ is younger than ⧠ .

12 What's the role of a mother? What do you expect a good mother to do? Discuss in groups.

 13 Listen and read. How long do orang-utans stay with their mums?

CONTENT WORDS

behaviour   give birth   jaws   mammal
maternal instinct   offspring   powerful   sight

Animal Mothers

1   Mothers are very special people. They not only give birth but they look after their children until they're old enough to take care of themselves. Mothers don't stop caring about their children even when they're adults. They want to know that they are healthy, happy and safe. Like humans, animals have got a maternal instinct, too. There are many similarities as well as differences in the way they look after their offspring.

2   Does your mum drive you to school, your music lesson or sports practice? Can you imagine your mother carrying you and your brothers and sisters on her back all the time? That's what a Surinam toad mum, a species of toad that comes from South America, does when she has babies. A Surinam toad mother carries as many as 100 babies on her back until they're old enough to swim by themselves.

3   Does your mum tell you to tidy your room and make your bed? Not if you're an orang-utan! Mother orang-utans from Indonesia are the only animal mothers who make a new place for their babies to sleep in each night. They collect fresh leaves, twigs and branches and build their young a bed high in the trees. Mums never let their babies out of their sight for the first two years and after that they keep them close until they're six or seven years old. This is longer than any other mammal spends raising its offspring, except humans.

4   The world can be a scary and dangerous place when you're young, even if you're an alligator. That's why mother alligators keep their young in their mouth while they're moving through water or other dangerous places. In the past, when people saw this, they thought the mother was eating her own babies! She's actually protecting them from predators when she's carrying them in her powerful jaws.

5   These are just a few examples of maternal behaviour among animals. One thing is certain – without mums to care and protect their offspring, every species on this planet would be endangered!

14 Look at 13 and say true or false.

1 Only human mothers have got a maternal instinct.

2 A Surinam toad mum can carry all her babies on her back at the same time.

3 Only orang-utan mothers build a new bed for their babies to sleep in each night.

4 Orang-utans sleep on soft beds of leaves under the trees.

5 In the past, alligator mums sometimes ate their babies.

6 Most animals could easily survive even without a mother to look after them.

15 Play a memory game in groups. Close your books. One person asks questions. The first one to answer correctly gets one point.

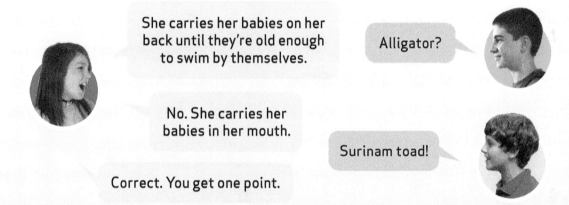

She carries her babies on her back until they're old enough to swim by themselves.

Alligator?

No. She carries her babies in her mouth.

Surinam toad!

Correct. You get one point.

16 Make an Animal Mothers poster. Then present it to the class.

Elephant Mothers

All female elephants help raise an elephant baby.

Elephant mothers are pregnant for 22 months. It's the longest pregnancy for any animal. When the baby is born, all the female elephants in the group help to take care of it.

Grammar

 17 Look, listen and read. Did Joy use to watch cartoons?

Mark and his sister, Joy, are watching TV.

Mark: Oh, great! Cartoons!

Joy: Boring! Can we watch something else?

Mark: But you used to love cartoons!

Joy: No, I didn't use to like watching cartoons.

Mark: What do you mean? Didn't we use to watch cartoons every day when we were on holiday?

Joy: Well, only because there was nothing else on TV.

18 Read and complete.

used to		
+	I ¹ 💡 **to** like cartoons when I was younger. She **used** ² 💡 watch cartoons with her brother.	
–	I ³ 💡 **use to** like action films but I love them now. He **didn't** ⁴ 💡 **to** see his cousins very often because he lived abroad.	
?	**Did** you ⁵ 💡 **to** watch cartoons on TV when you were five? ⁶ 💡 Pablo **use to** play basketball at university?	
	Yes, I **did**. / No, I ⁷ 💡 .	

19 Look at 18. Complete the sentences using used to and the words in brackets.

1 When I lived in the village, I 💡 to school.   (cycle)

2 You 💡 chocolate cake. Why don't you like it anymore?   (like)

3 My uncle Tom 💡 in a rock band.   (be)

4 They 💡 a lot before they had children.   (travel)

5 Dad 💡 in the city but now he works from home.   (work)

6 Anita 💡 at night very often when she was a baby.   (wake up)

20 Look at the information about Joy's family and write sentences with used/didn't use to.

	3 years ago	**now**
we	live in a small flat	live in a house with a garden
Mum	ride a motorbike	drive a car
Dad	have a wild beard	shave every day
my brother	play with blocks	watch cartoons
Aunt Kathy	work in a bank	own a cake shop
I	have piano lessons	play the guitar

Three years ago…

1 *They didn't use to live in a house with a garden. They used to live in a small flat.*

21 Work with a partner. Ask and answer. Write yes or no.

	10 years ago	**now**
Name: ?		
play sports?		
go to bed after midnight?		
tidy your room?		
go out with your friends?		

Did you use to play sports ten years ago?

No, I didn't. I was only two years old.

How about now?

I play hockey.

22 Look at the chart in 21 and tell the class what you know about your partner.

Max didn't use to play sports ten years ago but he does now. He plays hockey.

Special Days for Families

1   All around the world, families celebrate special days together. Traditions for these days are as different as the countries and the people who celebrate them. Some of these traditions may surprise you.

2   Getting married is one of the most important days in the lives of many people around the world. In Germany, the friends and family of the bride and groom gather a day before the wedding. They break dishes, flower pots, bottles and plates. Then the young couple has to clean it all up! This tradition is called polterabend. Germans believe that it brings good luck to the new couple. Cleaning up the mess together, also symbolises that they'll have to work together through the good and bad times in their life.

3   Families in most countries have a special day to celebrate mothers. In Serbia, this day is the second Sunday before Christmas. On that day, children sneak into their mother's bedroom and tie her feet together with ribbon so that she can't get out of bed. Then they shout, "Mother's Day, Mother's Day! What will you pay to get away?" Then the mother gives them small treats and presents as payment so that her children 'free' her.

23 Which days are special for your family? How do you celebrate them? Discuss in groups.

35

24 Listen and read. Which paragraph talks about: a Birthdays, b Weddings, c Mother's Day?

> **CONTENT WORDS**
> into   respectively   ribbon   sneak   stuff   symbolise   tradition   treat

25 Complete the sentences. Use words from the text.
1 Polterabend takes place the ❓ the wedding.
2 To show that they'll work together in life, the couple have to ❓ the mess.
3 In Serbia, the children ❓ their mum's ❓ together to keep her on the bed.
4 They only let their mum get up if she gives them ❓ and ❓.
5 The traditional food for a Chinese birthday party is ❓.
6 Chinese women chop up and throw away ❓ to avoid bad luck.

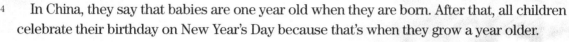

4   In China, they say that babies are one year old when they are born. After that, all children celebrate their birthday on New Year's Day because that's when they grow a year older. Actual birthdays are usually celebrated with a big family meal. The tradition is that the 'birthday boy' or 'birthday girl' should stuff their mouth with as many long noodles as they can and then eat them. This is because, in Chinese culture, long noodles symbolise a long life.

5   Some birthdays aren't celebrated at all because the Chinese believe they bring bad luck. On their 33rd and 66th birthdays, instead of celebrating, women buy a piece of meat and chop it up into 33 and 66 pieces respectively. Then they throw the meat away to make the bad luck go away, too. Also, to avoid bad luck, instead of turning 30 if they're women or 40 if they're men, they stay 29 and 39 for one more year!

26 Work with a partner. Choose a card. Ask and answer questions about each other's celebrations.

Student A

Celebration	Chinese New Year
Where	China
When	It's on a different day each year, between 21 January and 20 February.
What people do ?	People visit friends and family. They hang gold and red decorations. Gold brings wealth and red brings good luck. They have a very big festive dinner on New Year's Eve.

Student B

Celebration	Family Day
Where	Australia
When	First Monday in September
What people do ?	People take a day off work to spend time with their families. They do various family activities. They go on mini family vacations.

What's the name of the celebration?

It's the Chinese New Year.

27 Write about a special day in your country and how your family celebrates it.

THINK BIG Do you think traditional celebrations are important for cultural reasons? Why?

28 Read Rosie's story.

My Story
by Rosie Harris

I was born in 2003. My family lived in Islington, London. When I was a year old, my family moved to St Albans. There were just three of us then: my mum, my dad and me. Two years later, we moved to Nottingham. We lived there until 2010. By then, I had two younger brothers. We needed a bigger house! So when I was seven, we moved to Peterborough. A few months ago, we went back to visit our old neighbourhood in Nottingham. I saw my old house. It looked even smaller than I remembered! Our family and our house are much bigger now!

29 Copy and complete the chart with information from the story in 28.

When?	What happened?
2003	I was born. We lived in Islington, London.
2004	
	We moved to Nottingham.
2010	
A few months ago	

30 Copy the chart into your notebook and complete it with information about your life so far. Then use it to write a story about you.

When?	What happened?

31 Work in a small group. Take turns reading your stories. What's the same? What's different?

32 What kind of family traditions do you have? Copy, read and ✔. Add one tradition of your own. Then ask a partner.

Tradition	You	Your partner
1 We visit our relatives on special holidays.		
2 We have a special meal on family birthdays.		
3 We have a family night at home every week.		
4		

PROJECT

33 Make a page for a class book about family traditions.

1 Include a drawing or a picture of your favourite family tradition.

2 Write a short description about it.

3 Share your page with the class.

My family has family night every Thursday.

Two years ago, we started a new family tradition. We have family night every Thursday night. We all make time to be together. Last week, we played a board game. I lost but it was fun.

THINK BIG What's your favourite family tradition?
Why are family traditions important?

34 Listen, read and repeat.

1 g-e   ge   **2** g-i   gi   **3** g-y   gy

 35 Listen and blend the sounds.

1 g-e-l   gel   **2** g-i-n-g-er   ginger

3 g-y-m   gym   **4** g-y-p-s-y   gypsy

5 g-i-r-a-ffe giraffe   **6** g-e-m   gem

 36 Listen and chant.

A ginger giraffe
Worked out in a gym.
Quick! Get him some gel
For his hair!

37 Complete the story. Make up the information.

Aunt Isobel

Aunt Isobel is a very interesting person. She was born in 🔲 but her family moved to 🔲 when she was 🔲 years old. When she was in 🔲 school, she had a collection of 🔲 . It was probably the 🔲 collection of 🔲 in the world. People came from all over the world to see it. Now Aunt Isobel is 🔲 years old and she lives in 🔲 with 🔲 .

38 Take turns asking your classmates about their Aunt Isobel stories.

1 Where was Aunt Isobel born?   **2** When did her family move?

3 Where did they go?   **4** What kind of collection did Aunt Isobel have?

5 Why was the collection special?   **6** How old is Aunt Isobel now?

7 Where does she live now?   **8** Who does she live with?

39 Complete the sentences. Use the correct form of the verb.

> be born   get married   graduate   move

1 My favourite aunt ? from university two years ago.

2 In 2007, his grandparents ? to Bristol.

3 When Celia's brother ?, she was five years old.

4 Our parents ? 15 years ago.

40 Complete the dialogue. Use the correct form of used to and the words in brackets.

Anna: Who's that?

Ben: That's a picture of my grandma. She graduated from university this year. She always ¹? (say) that she would get a degree one day.

Anna: That's amazing!

Ben: Yes, it is. She didn't have time for university when she was younger. She ²? (love) school though and that's why she decided to start studying for her degree a few years ago.

Anna: ³? (she read) a lot before university?

Ben: Yes, she did. But she ⁴? (not read) textbooks. She ⁵? (prefer) novels.

 I Can

- talk about important life events and habits of the past.
- make comparisons.

unit 3

HELPING OTHERS

Read about how children are helping others. Answer the questions with a partner. Then listen and check.

1   **Cupcakes for Cancer** Thirteen-year-old Blakely Colvin had a friend with leukemia, a kind of cancer. Blakely wanted to help her ill friend. What could she do? She decided to sell cupcakes after school. She sold her cupcakes for 50p each and, with the help of friends, they raised £1,800 in six weeks.

   On average, how many cupcakes did Blakely and her friends bake every day?

2   **Creative Children for Charity** Chirag Vedullapalli wanted to do something to help others. He always loved to paint and draw. When he was nine years old, he decided he could sell his artwork and donate the money to a local children's hospital in Seattle, Washington, a big city on the west coast of the USA. Chirag's friends loved the idea, too. Chirag and ten of his friends each created one piece of art. They sold them for £10 each.

   How much money did Chirag and his friends raise for the children's hospital?

3   **Biking for America** When Joseph Machado was 13 years old, he decided he could help children who are less fortunate and could do what he likes best, too – bike riding. He created Biking for America. Joseph rode his bike from California to Washington, DC, raising money along the way. Joseph rode his bike 120 kilometres a day for 39 days.

   In total, how many kilometres did Joseph ride?

2 Read. Use the words from the boxes to complete the sentences. Then listen and check.

A The school choir is entering a big singing competition. The choir wants to buy new outfits for it. They need to raise money to buy them. Listen to their ideas:

> art fair   cake sale   concert

Fundraising		
1 We could have a/an ❓. We could sell biscuits, pies and cakes.	**2** We could have a/an ❓. Local artists could exhibit and sell their work.	**3** We could have a/an ❓. We could perform songs and dances with a specific theme.

B The choir has ideas for how to advertise their fundraising activities. Listen.

> article   posters   video

Advertising		
1 We're going to design colourful ❓ and hang them up around school.	**2** I'm going to write a/an ❓ about our activities for the school newspaper.	**3** I'm going to make a/an ❓ of the choir performing and post it on the school website.

3 Work with a partner. Ask and answer.

What could they do to raise money?

They could bake cakes and sell them.

What are they going to do to tell people about it?

They're going to make posters and hang them up around school.

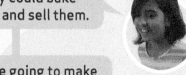

THINK BIG What else could they do to raise money?
How else could they advertise their fundraising activities?

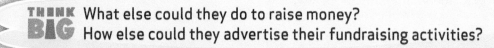

4 Listen and read. What did wburrington suggest?

◀ ▶ ⟳ ⌂ ✕ + www.dentonschool.org   🔍

Denton School Blog

On Wednesday 15th April at 1:37 p.m., Mr Thompson wrote...

FUNDRAISING TIME!

The Sports Department is asking pupils in years 7–10 to help out with this year's fundraising activities. We're going to use the money to help pay for new equipment, refreshments after matches and trips to matches at other schools.

If you've got any ideas for fundraising activities, please post them in the comments section below.

COMMENTS

cromano said
We could sell chocolate bars. Who doesn't like chocolate?

rmcnally said
I like chocolates! Let's have a cake sale. We could sell chocolate cake, brownies and chocolate chip cookies. I'm getting hungry!

wburrington said
We could have a dance. My brother's class did that at his secondary school and they made a lot of money.

jharmon said
Yes, we could make something, like T-shirts with the name of our school on them. And then we could sell them on the school website.

lscott said
I've got a good idea! Why don't we have a 5 km fun run around the town? It could end on our school sports field and we could charge an entry fee and sell our school T-shirts, too.

tjameson said
At my junior school, we had a basketball shoot-out to raise money. Children had to pay to shoot ten balls and the person with the best score in each class got a prize. It was such fun!

(Login) to add your comment below.

www.dentonschool.org

On Monday 20th April at 9:02 a.m., Mr Thompson wrote...

FUNDRAISING UPDATE

Thanks for all the great ideas! The sports teachers and I discussed all the ideas you gave us and a few other ones. Here's the fundraising plan that we came up with for this year:

- Year 7: You're going to sell chocolate bars. We're going to order them from Charlie's Chocolates. They cost 50p each. Mr Campbell, the basketball teacher, is going to give you more information on Thursday.
- Year 8: You're going to sell water bottles with our school name and logo on them. The bottles cost £2.50 each. Miss Carpenter, the tennis teacher, is going to tell you more about it tomorrow after lunch.
- Year 9: You're going to have a dance and sell tickets to it. It's going to be in the school hall on Saturday night, 8th May. Ms Richards and Mr Benson, the football coaches, are going to meet you in the cafeteria next Tuesday before lunch to talk more about it.
- Year 10: You're going to have a cake sale. Mrs Fenton, the school nurse, is going to meet you this Friday, in the Year 10 common room, to give you more information.

We're all looking forward to this year's fundraising events. We know they're going to be a big success!

READING COMPREHENSION

5 Answer the questions with a partner.

1 What fundraising ideas did pupils post?

2 What is each year going to do to raise money?

6 Find words in 4 with these meanings.

1 collecting money for a specific reason

2 items you need for a specific activity

3 drinks and snacks

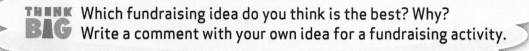

THINK BIG Which fundraising idea do you think is the best? Why?
Write a comment with your own idea for a fundraising activity.

7 Listen and read. What are the raffle winners going to get?

Vicky:	Let's talk about how we're going to raise money for our class trip. Any ideas?
Tanya:	I've got an idea. We could all make something to sell.
Vicky:	Like what?
Tanya:	Well, we all like art. I like painting, you're good at sculpture and Susie likes taking photos…
Caroline:	So we could have an art exhibition here at the school.
Tanya:	Yes!
Vicky:	Wait a minute. Are people really going to buy our things? I'm not so sure.
Caroline:	Well, we could sell tickets to the exhibition. You know, raffle tickets.
Vicky:	Oh, I see. We sell raffle tickets and we pick the winners at the exhibition. The winners take home the art!
Tanya:	That sounds like a good idea! Let's tell the class.

8 Practise the dialogue in 7 with a partner.

9 Listen and answer the questions.

1 What could she do?

2 What are they going to do?

3 What's he going to do?

4 What could she do?

| How **could** we raise money for our club? | We **could** have a car wash. |
| How much **could** they charge to wash one car? | They **could** charge €10 for a small car. For a bigger car, they **could** charge €15. |

Tip: Use *could* to express possibility or make suggestions.

10 Complete the questions. Use how could or what could plus one of the words or phrases from the box.

> do to help   help people   make   raise money   tell people

1 **A:** ❓ we ❓ about the drama club?
  B: We could make posters.

2 **A:** ❓ they ❓ in their community?
  B: They could clean up the town park.

3 **A:** ❓ she ❓ us at the cake sale?
  B: She could put the icing on the cupcakes.

4 **A:** ❓ they ❓ for new equipment?
  B: They could have an art fair and sell their art work.

5 **A:** ❓ I ❓ for the art fair?
  B: You could make a collage.

| **Are** you **going to have** a concert? | Yes, we **are**. |
| How **are you going to tell** people about it? | We**'re going to make** posters. |

Tip: Use *is/am/are going to* to talk about events in the future.

11 Complete the sentences with the correct form of be + going to.

Lisa: Our football team ¹❓ have a cake sale next week.

Paul: Really? ²❓ you ❓ bake something?

Lisa: Uh… no. I'm not into baking.

Paul: So what ³❓ you ❓ do to help?

Lisa: I ⁴❓ write an article for the school website.

12 Can you remember any advertisements you saw lately? What do you think makes these particular advertisements easier to remember than others? Discuss in groups.

 13 Listen and read. What makes a brilliant ad?

> **CONTENT WORDS**
> bold   effective   focus   get across   image   impatient   invisible   layout

Creating an Effective Advertisement

1   What makes an advertisement effective? You can easily answer this question if you walk around a city. There are thousands of advertisements but which ones catch your eye? A good ad (short for advertisement) is one that gets your attention. If it makes you focus on the important information, too, it does its job very well. Lastly, if you still remember the message after you move on, then it's a brilliant ad!

2   To learn how to create an effective ad, like a poster for example, start by comparing the two posters on the right. Answer this without stopping to think: Which one is more effective? Yes, it's the one at the bottom. Let's examine why.

3   First of all, it's more colourful and it's got attractive pictures. The white and black poster almost becomes invisible next to it. Colour draws attention. Moreover, it can affect your mood and make you react in a certain way. The colour red excites you and makes you feel bold and adventurous. The colour blue makes you believe that what you're reading is true. Images do the same. Do the cupcakes on the poster at the bottom of the page make your mouth water? Do they make you scan the text to find out where you can get them? That's what they're there for!

4   An ad isn't just colour and pictures. You've got something to say, so the next thing you should do is decide how much text you should write. Remember that people are impatient and will rarely read a long text to see what it's about. The amount of text should be just right to get your message across, so focus on your message and say it with as few words as possible. Your choice of font (the style of letters), font size (how big or small the letters are) and font colour also play an important role. You want the text to be easy to read, especially from a distance.

5   Finally, you have to decide how you're going to organise both the pictures and the text in the space you've got. A good layout helps people 'read' the ad quickly and communicates your message more effectively. If your poster is too busy, your message will simply get lost!

CAKE SALE

Come to the gym today between 12–2 p.m. The school karate club is selling cupcakes to raise money for a field trip.

Enjoy a delicious cupcake for only 50p and support your school karate club!

CAKE SALE

Help the karate club raise money for a field trip. Enjoy a delicious cupcake today for only 50p!

Time:
12:00–2:00 p.m.

Place:
School gym

14 Look at 13. Choose the correct words.

1 We know that an ad is effective when it makes us **notice it/compare it with others**.

2 The black and white poster doesn't work because **we can't see it/it doesn't draw our attention**.

3 Different colours make us **feel more adventurous/think differently**.

4 Images make us **notice the advertisement more/feel hungry**.

5 Most people **haven't got the time to read/don't want to read** long texts in an ad.

6 People should be able to see what's in a poster even when **they're far away/the message is lost**.

15 Complete the checklist.

How to create an effective poster

1 Choose bright ? to draw attention to the poster.

2 Use colourful and attractive ? to illustrate it.

3 Focus on your ? . Make sure what you're saying is clear.

4 Write the right amount of ? – not too long, not too short.

5 Choose the right ? style, size and colour.

6 Make sure the ? is good. Don't make the poster too busy.

16 Work with a partner. Make a poster for a fundraising event at your school.

Begin by deciding the details of the event. You can get ideas from page 39 or use your own. Discuss all the steps in the checklist in 15 and make decisions. Take notes.

Background:

Text: Font: size   colour

Text content:

Pictures:

Layout:

I think we should use blue text on a yellow background.

I like blue for the text but I'm not sure about yellow. How about orange?

Grammar

17 Look, listen and read. Has George ever been fishing?

Zac: I'm going fishing with my dad this weekend.

George: That sounds fun!

Zac: Honestly? Have you ever been fishing?

George: No, I haven't. Why?

Zac: I've spent endless hours sitting in a boat and believe me, it's the most boring thing in the world!

George: I think I'd like it. Anyway, I'm going rock climbing with my cousins. I've never done it before but I'm sure I won't enjoy it. I hate heights!

Zac: I've never been rock climbing either but I'd love to! Hey, why don't we swap? You go fishing with my dad and I'll go rock climbing with your cousins!

George: It's a deal!

Present Perfect for experiences	
+	I**'ve spent** endless hours sitting in a boat.
	My dad **has caught** lots of fish.
-	I**'ve** never **done** it before./**I haven't done** it before.
	He**'s** never **been** rock climbing./He **hasn't been** rock climbing.
?	**Have** you ever **been** fishing?
	Yes, I **have**./No, I **haven't**.

have been / have gone
I**'ve been** to London. = I'm back now.
She**'s gone** to London. = She's still there.

18 Say what experiences these people have had. Then write the sentences in the negative in your notebook.

1   Emilio 🕃 a tall mountain.   **climb**

2   Jade 🕃 on a boat.   **sail**

3   We 🕃 an effective poster.   **create**

19 Copy the chart in your notebook. Complete using the words from the box.

> been   bought   caught   driven   drunk   eaten   found
> had   made   met   read   ridden   seen   written

Infinitive		Simple Past		Past Participle	
be	meet	was/were	met		
have	find	had	found		
make	write	made	wrote		
see	read	saw	read		
eat	drive	ate	drove		
drink	ride	drank	rode		
catch	buy	caught	bought		

20 Work with a partner. Ask and answer. Give true answers.

1 meet somebody famous?
2 go to Europe?
3 watch a scary film?
4 finish all levels in a video game?
5 see an elephant in real life?
6 act in a school play?

Have you ever met somebody famous?

Yes, I have.

21 Write what your partner has/hasn't done.

> *Cesar hasn't met anybody famous. He's never been to Europe. But he has*
>
> *watched a few scary films and he's acted in a school play.*

Doing What You Can

Not all the people in the world have the good fortune to have good health, a roof over their head or enough food to eat. Also, many animals are left in the streets hungry, cold and helpless because their owners don't want to look after them anymore. Both people and animals need a helping hand and charity groups are there to offer it. There are many different charity organisations all over the world that help people and animals in need – and they rely on the work of volunteers to raise money for their cause. Many young people raise money for charity. Read about what these young people from around the world are doing.

1
Dublin, Ireland

Libby Mulligan loves to play the guitar and sing – and people love to listen to her. When she was 12 years old, she decided that she could play her guitar and sing at parties and weddings for money. Libby may not be a professional musician but she earns enough money to donate to a children's cancer charity in her community.

22 How does your community deal with people and animals in need? Which groups and organisations help them? How? Discuss with a partner.

23 Listen and read. Match the titles A–C to the paragraphs 1–3.

 A Art for animals

 B A lesson to learn

 C A song from the heart

> **CONTENT WORDS**
> animal shelter   benefit   cancer   cause
> donate   fortune   proof   raise   rescue
> supplies   tutoring   volunteer

24 Correct the mistakes. Write new sentences.

 1 Charity organisations pay people to raise money for their cause.

 2 Playing the guitar and singing at weddings and parties is Libby's job.

 3 Charles wrote a letter to the animal shelter to ask why they weren't doing anything about stray animals.

 4 Charles sells his illustrations at charity events.

 5 Tandi and Stefan offer their tutoring services to homeless children.

2
Paris, France

Charles Lyon is a young artist who sells his art online to raise money for animal rescue. It all started when Charles wrote a letter to a local animal shelter asking what he could do to help stray cats and dogs in his neighbourhood. Then he came up with his website idea. Charles draws and sells pictures of animals on it. So far, he has sold more than 200 illustrations. He donates the money to local animal shelters and organisations that help find stray animals a new home.

3
Cape Town, South Africa

Tandi Jacobs and Stefan Burg wanted to help homeless children in their city. They decided to raise money by offering tutoring services. They used the money they earned to buy blankets, food and other supplies. More than 1,000 others have joined them, benefitting homeless children in other places around the country.

The work these young people do has made a difference to the lives of people around them. They're the proof that if we all do a little, we can achieve great things.

25 Discuss with a partner. Read the information about these International Charity Organisations. Which one would you like to volunteer for? Why? Then write in your notebook.

Best Friends Shelter	
What	Help care for rescue animals, i.e. clean their living space, feed and walk them
Where	Europe (10 countries, including France, the U.K., Italy and Spain)
Skills needed	English, experience with pets

Make a gift Organisation	
What	Collect money and supplies for families in need
Where	Anywhere in the world, including your country
Skills needed	No specific skills but volunteers need to be enthusiastic and invest a lot of their time

I would like to volunteer for *Best Friends Shelter* because I speak English and I've got experience with pets.

I'd like to volunteer for *Make a Gift Organisation*. I'm enthusiastic and I've got a lot of spare time!

THINK BIG What international charity groups and organisations do you know? What kind of problem do you think you could help with? How?

26 Read Michael's letter to his head teacher.

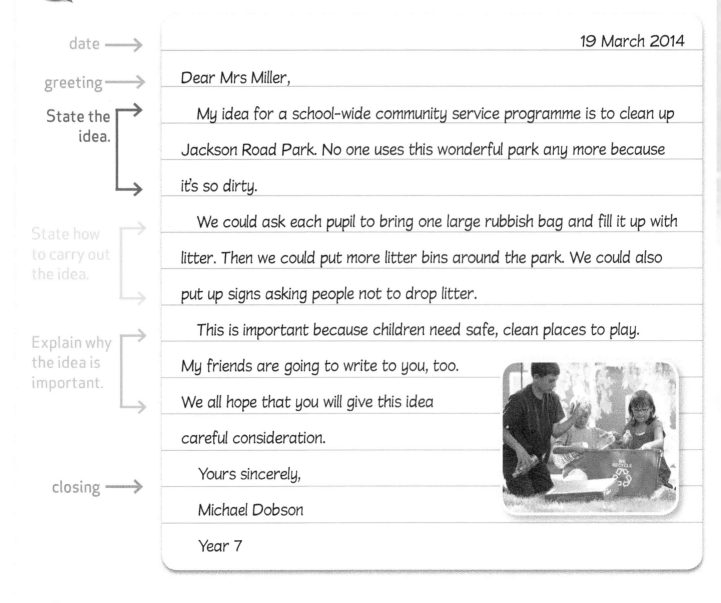

date →

19 March 2014

greeting →

Dear Mrs Miller,

State the idea. →

My idea for a school-wide community service programme is to clean up Jackson Road Park. No one uses this wonderful park any more because it's so dirty.

State how to carry out the idea. →

We could ask each pupil to bring one large rubbish bag and fill it up with litter. Then we could put more litter bins around the park. We could also put up signs asking people not to drop litter.

Explain why the idea is important. →

This is important because children need safe, clean places to play. My friends are going to write to you, too. We all hope that you will give this idea careful consideration.

closing →

Yours sincerely,

Michael Dobson

Year 7

27 What kind of school-wide community service programmes could you suggest to your head teacher? Discuss with a partner.

We could visit elderly people in a care home.

And we could visit ill children in a hospital.

28 Choose one of your ideas and write a letter to your head teacher. Describe your idea and explain why it's important.

29 Look at the names of the international charity groups. Match the name of the charity group to the description of the group.

a UNICEF b Médecins Sans Frontières (Doctors Without Borders) c Room to Read® d WWF

1 This international group sends doctors and nurses to help people in almost 70 countries around the world.

2 This organisation builds libraries and gives books to children in many different countries across Asia and Africa.

3 This group, part of the United Nations, works for the rights of children, including their rights to education, food, clean water and medical care.

4 This conservation group works to protect the future of nature and animals. It's got more than five million supporters around the world.

PROJECT

30 Work in a small group. How could you raise money for a charity group? Write a fundraising plan. Then create an advert.

Fundraising Plan

Goal: Raise €100 for animal shelter
Activity: School cake sale
What: Biscuits and cupcakes
Where: School playground
When: Next Monday lunchtime
How: Create an advert

Idea for advert:
Your local animal shelter needs you.
Help homeless animals find a good home!
Enjoy a delicious cupcake after lunch for only 50¢!
Time: 12–2 p.m. next Monday
Place: School playground

THINK BIG Which of the charities in 29 is the most interesting to you? Why? How could you help one of these groups?

53

31 Listen, read and repeat.

1 l-k   lk   2 m-b   mb

 54

32 Listen and blend the sounds.

1 w-a-lk   walk   2 c-o-mb   comb

3 l-a-mb   lamb   4 t-a-lk   talk

5 c-l-i-mb   climb   6 ch-a-lk   chalk

 55

33 Listen and chant.

A lamb can walk
But a lamb can't talk.
A lamb is the colour of white chalk!

34 Read the blog and comments. Follow the instructions. Discuss your choices with a partner. What else could you do?

 www.dentonschool.org

HELP BEAUTIFY OUR SCHOOL!

The art club needs your help! We're going to make our school beautiful this month. We've got to be resourceful and use what we've got on hand, such as basic art supplies. We haven't got money to spend. Look at these ideas people have suggested and choose the best ones. Remember, if it costs money, we probably can't do it.

Comments
- We could make a mural and hang it outside the office.
- We could replace the old office door.
- We could paint the old office door.
- We could organise the noticeboard and make it look more attractive.
- We could put some green plants in the hall.
- We could plant some flowers in front of the school.

35 Read and complete.

1 Your school band wants to raise money to buy some new drums.
What could you do? Write three ideas.

We could…

2 Which idea is the best one? Why?

I think…

3 Write three ways to tell people about your fundraising event. Use complete sentences.

We're going to…

36 Read the poster and the sponsorship form. Say what these people have done to support the walkathlon.

THANK YOU FOR SUPPORTING OUR WALKATHON!

More than 100 participants, old and young, walked from 1 to 10 km, raising over €5,000 for Families in Need.

Our sponsors made it possible. Thank you.

Sponsors

1	Mrs Madison	give €2 for every kilometre her friend walks
2	Jessie Kincaide	walk 5 kilometres in the Walkathon
3	Emma Smith	offer €3 for every kilometre my sister walks

I Can

- talk about helping others and about fundraising activities.
- talk about possibilities and experiences.
- say what I'm going to do.

How Well Do I Know It? Can I Use It?

1 Think about it. Read and draw. Practise.

😊 I know this.　　😐 I need more practice.　　☹ I don't know this.

	PAGES			
Activities: basketball team, drama club, school orchestra…	5	😊	😐	☹
Life events: was born, got married, graduated…	21	😊	😐	☹
Fundraising activities: have a cake sale, sell tickets, have an art fair…	37	😊	😐	☹
Advertising: make a poster, write an article, make a video…	37	😊	😐	☹
How about **joining** the school news bloggers? I'm interested in **writing** articles. She's good at **acting**.	8–9	😊	😐	☹
She **comes** from China. They**'re talking** on the phone now. I **did** my homework yesterday.	12–13	😊	😐	☹
My family moved **when I was five**. He graduated **six years ago**.	24–25	😊	😐	☹
I **used to** swim but I don't anymore. **Did** she **use to** study a lot? You **didn't use to** play basketball.	28–29	😊	😐	☹
How **could** we raise money for our school outing? We **could** have a cake sale.	40–41	😊	😐	☹
What **are** you **going to do** for the cake sale? I**'m going to bake** some biscuits.	40–41	😊	😐	☹
Have you ever **been** fishing? Yes, I **have**. I **haven't done** it before. I**'ve been** to London many times. She**'s gone** to Paris on holiday.	44–45	😊	😐	☹

I Can Do It!

56

2 **Get ready.**

A Complete the dialogue with the correct form of the verbs. Then listen and check.

Mrs Rogers: Everyone, I've got news. Do you remember Mr Finnegan?

Sandra: Yes. He ¹ (be) our music teacher. He was one of the best teachers we ² (ever have)!

Jack: Yes, I ³ (use to) have violin lessons with him when I ⁴ (be) six.

Mrs Rogers: Well, Mr Finnegan ⁵ (retire) at the end of this school year. The head teacher ⁶ (want) us to think of something we can do for him. Any ideas?

Will: I've got one. Everyone could ⁷ (write) a poem about Mr Finnegan. How about ⁸ (put) them all together in a book?

Sandra: I don't know. I like ⁹ (read) poems but I'm not good at ¹⁰ (write) them.

Jack: I like ¹¹ (write) poems. But I've got another idea. I think we should ¹² (take) a lot of photos around the school and we should ¹³ (put) them on a big poster.

Will: Good idea! We could ¹⁴ (write) funny notes next to the photos. Mr Finnegan would like that!

B Practise the dialogue in **A** with a partner.

C Ask and answer the questions with a partner.

1 What could the pupils write poems about?

2 What could the pupils take photos of?

3 Which idea do you think is better – the book of poems or the poster?

3 **Get set.**

 STEP 1 Cut out the cards on page 159 of your Activity Book.

 STEP 2 Divide the cards into two sets: *A* cards in one set and *B* cards in another. Now you're ready to **Go!**

4 **Go!**

A Look at the pictures. Make a dialogue for each picture using the *A* and *B* cards.

Dialogue 1: Amanda and Kerry

Dialogue 2: Jacob and Thomas

B Practise the two dialogues with a partner.

C Now make up your own dialogue. Choose one of these situations. Role play your dialogue in front of another pair.

Situation 1:

Pupil A	Pupil B
You're new at this school and you want to join a club.	You and your brother play sports. You're in several clubs at school, too. Give your new friend advice.

Situation 2:

Pupil A	Pupil B
You're moving to another town soon. You're upset about moving.	You moved to this town when you were little. You remember how you felt when you moved. Give your friend advice.

5 Write about yourself in your notebook.

- Do you play sports at school or are you a member of a club?
- What kinds of things are you interested in doing in your free time?
- When did you start going to your current school?
- What school are you going to go to after this one?
- Have you ever visited another school that you liked?

All About Me Date:_____

_____

_____

1

2

3

4

5

How Well Do I Know It Now?

6 Look at page 52 and your notebook. Draw again.

A Use a different colour.

B Read and think.

I can start the next unit.

I can ask my teacher for help and then start the next unit.

I can practise and then start the next unit.

7 Rate this Checkpoint.

 very easy   easy   hard   very hard   fun   OK   not fun

6

7

8

9

Units 1–3 Exam Preparation

What did each person do at the weekend?
Listen and write a letter in each box. There is one example.

Judy ☐ D

Sarah ☐

Paul ☐

Tony ☐

Adam ☐

Ben ☐

A

B

C

D

E

F

G

H

Read the story. Choose a word from the box. Write the correct word next to numbers 1–6. There is one example.

    My name's Seb and I've got a cat called Molly. She's beautiful. She's _____small_____ and black and very naughty. Molly is good at (1) _____ trees. Two weeks ago, I lost Molly. I looked in the house, in the garden and in the park but I couldn't find her. I was very worried because Molly didn't come home for her dinner and she loves her (2) _____ . I went into the garden and then I had an idea. Where does Molly like to go? She's always in the tall tree in our garden. I looked up and Molly was on the top of the tree. I shouted to Molly but she was asleep and she didn't hear me. I shouted again, "Molly, Molly!" Then, she woke up but she (3) _____ get down from the tree. I ran inside the house and told my dad that Molly was in the tree. My dad is very tall and strong. He tried to climb the tree but he couldn't because it's very high. So my dad put a (4) _____ under the tree. He put me on his shoulders and he climbed onto the table. I lifted Molly out of the tree and we all went back for our dinner. I gave Molly her (5) _____ food that evening!

Example				
small	table	food	walk	climbing
under	saw	couldn't	high	favourite

(6) Now choose the best name for the story.

    Tick one box.

        Molly loves her dinner   ☐

        Molly's best day   ☐

        The day I lost Molly   ☐

unit 4 SHOPPING AROUND

58

1 Read. Guess the answer to each question. Then listen and check.

1 What's an oniomaniac?

    a Someone who shops too much.

    b Someone who is afraid of shopping.

    c Someone who eats too many onions.

2 People in Banjarmasin, in Indonesia, get up early to buy their food. The market is open from 5:00 to 9:00 in the morning. The market sells fresh fruit, vegetables, fish, cakes and many other things. Why is this market more interesting than others?

    a There are no shops.

    b The sellers are all in boats!

    c Both a and b.

3 The Dubai Mall in Dubai, United Arab Emirates, is the largest shopping centre in the world and has got the world's biggest sweet shop. It's also one of the most popular shopping centres in the world. How many people visited this shopping centre in 2011?

    a 12 million

    b 54 million

    c 97 million

2 Michelle and Dylan are talking about buying presents. What do they decide to buy? Listen and choose.

a beaded bracelet

a turquoise necklace

silver earrings

balloons

a picture frame

a bouquet of roses

3 Listen again and take notes. Then choose the correct answers.

1 Michelle is going to buy her present at ❓ in the shopping centre.

   a a clothes shop   **b** a jewellery shop   **c** a department store

2 Dylan is going to buy his present at ❓.

   a a card shop   **b** a flower shop   **c** a craft fair

4 Work with a partner. Ask and answer. Use your notes.

What does Michelle say about the silver earrings?

They're less expensive than the bracelet and they're beautiful.

THINK BIG Why do you think people give presents on Mother's Day? How else can you celebrate Mother's Day?

62

5 Listen and read. What's wrong with the earphones?

www.reviewsbykids.com

▶ TV Shows

▶ Films

▶ Books

▶ Clothes

▼ Gadgets

• Digital Cameras

• Headphones

• mp3 Players

• Video Games

REVIEWS BY KIDS
THE WEBSITE BY AND FOR KIDS

Click on any category. Read a review or write a review. It's up to you!

EAR PALS   £10.99
Average Rating ★ ★ ☆ ☆ ☆

REVIEWS

★ ☆ ☆ ☆ ☆ **Never again!**
By Tamsin (Norwich)

My mum gave me a gift voucher for an online shop. I decided to use it to buy a pair of these headphones. They're called Ear Pals. I don't like them! The cords are too long and there's no case like the one they showed online. They aren't as good as they looked, that's for sure! Plus, the Ear Pals keep falling out of my ears. Maybe my ears are the wrong shape? Or maybe the wrong size? I don't know. These 'earphones' are definitely NOT my pals! Read more reviews...

CAMO-PHONES   £20.95
Average Rating ★ ★ ★ ★ ☆

REVIEWS

★ ★ ★ ★ ★ **Fantastic!**
By muzik freak (Sheffield)

Good sound and great design. The camouflage design helps you hide when you're on a secret mission. They're a little expensive, it's true. But to me, they're worth the money. I used to buy less expensive headphones but they never lasted very long. Well, I learnt my lesson. Camo-Phones are the best. Read more reviews...

www.reviewsbykids.com

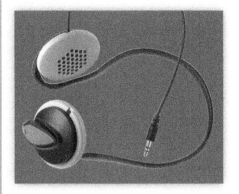

BIG SOUND WRAP-AROUNDS
$5.99
Average Rating ★ ★ ★ ☆ ☆

REVIEWS
★ ★ ★ ☆ ☆ **Good for the price**
By Danny

   OK, maybe these aren't the best headphones in the world. They're definitely not as good as my old ones but at least they work. And they're the least expensive ones I know. The sound is just OK. Not good, not bad. But they're really cheap.

Read more reviews...

READING COMPREHENSION

6 Answer the questions with a partner.

1 Which headphones are the most expensive?

2 Which headphones are the least expensive?

3 Which headphones got the best review?

4 Which headphones got the worst review?

THINK BIG Which headphones do you think give the best value for money? Why? Which headphones would you buy? Why? Why do you think people read product reviews?

Language in Action

7 Listen and read. Which game shop has got the cheapest prices?

Karen: What are you going to buy with your gift voucher?

Josh: A new game called Tunnel Island. I played it at Zach's house. It's really fun.

Karen: Great. So, where are you going to buy it?

Josh: That's what I'm trying to work out. I'm looking at prices online.

Karen: Good idea. Try looking at Game Time. No, wait. Look at Chester's. They're usually less expensive than Game Time.

Josh: Let me see… yes, you can find it at Chester's and it's only €25.00. I'm going to ask my mum to drive me there. Want to come?

Karen: OK.

8 Practise the dialogue in 7 with a partner.

9 Listen and find. Then choose a phrase from the box.

> a friend has got it   read an online review
> saw it in a magazine   saw it on TV

a

mp3
8GB
€70
FREE

b

SOLD OUT
4GB
€40
SALE
FREE

c

mp3
16GB
€100

d

mp3
8GB
€75

The blue shoes are **expensive**.	The white shoes are **less expensive than** the blue shoes.
The red shoes are **more expensive than** the blue shoes.	
The black shoes are **the most expensive** of all.	The white shoes are **the least expensive** of all.
The red shoes are not **as expensive as** the black shoes.	

10 Complete the sentences. Use the adjective in brackets and more … than or the most.

1 *Summer's End* looks 🔑 (interesting) *The Boys Are Back*.

2 *The Winning Game* is 🔑 (interesting) book in the shop.

3 *Up the Stairs* is 🔑 (exciting) of all the films here.

4 *Brain Power* is 🔑 (exciting) *Mountain Rescue*.

5 *Great Escape* is 🔑 (popular) *Find the Weasel*.

6 *Mind Bender* is 🔑 (popular) video game of all.

7 *Super Invaders* is 🔑 (expensive) *Spot the Alien*.

8 *Cowgirls* is 🔑 (expensive) DVD here.

11 Look at 10. Use as … as.

1 *The Boys Are Back* doesn't look 🔑 *Summer's End*.

2 *Mountain Rescue* isn't 🔑 *Brain Power*.

3 *Find the Weasel* isn't 🔑 *Great Escape*.

4 *Spot the Alien* isn't 🔑 *Super Invaders*.

The price of those trainers is **too** high.	The price isn't low **enough**.
Those jeans are **too** baggy.	The jeans aren't tight **enough**.

12 Make sentences in your notebook. Use too or enough and a word from each box.

board game coat curry sandals	comfortable expensive spicy warm

13 Is money more important than other things in life? Discuss in groups.

14 67 Listen and read. When were the first coins used?

CONTENT WORDS

bartering   bronze   coin   currency   exchange   grain   livestock   seal   trade

Money, Money, Money!

1   Most people today use coins, paper money or credit cards to buy things. However, shopping wasn't always as easy as that.

2   About 10,000 years ago, people farmed and grew the food they needed. They raised livestock, like cows and goats, and grew grain, like rice and wheat. During that time, people used bartering. This means they exchanged goods between them. They mostly used livestock and grain instead of money in many different parts of the world. It must have been quite tricky to decide the price of things. If we still used bartering, how many goats or sacks of grain would you have to give for a video game?

3   Over the years, things changed and, about 3,000 years ago, people started to use other things as money. Shells from the sea, for example, such as the cowrie shell, were traded as money in places like China, Thailand, India and some countries in Africa.

4   It wasn't until about 2,000 years ago when the first coins appeared. China, Greece and India were probably the first places to use metal coins. Most coins were made of expensive metals like bronze, silver or gold. They were made by heating small amounts of metal and then putting a seal on them (Greece) or putting a hole in the middle (India and China).

5   But carrying around a lot of heavy coins wasn't very practical. That's probably why paper money started to be used in China, almost 1,000 years ago. In Europe, paper money began as 'bank notes'. The first bank notes were made in Sweden, in 1661.

6   Almost every country has got its own currency (a specific kind of money). For example, the USA has got American dollars and the United Kingdom has got British pounds. We can tell how much one unit of a certain currency is worth in another currency. This is a very useful thing when you want to travel abroad!

7   As you see, what we use for money has changed quite a few times up to now and it's very likely to change in the future, too.

THINK BIG How do you think we'll pay for things in the future?

15 Look at 14. Complete the sentences.

1 When people used 🔟 , they gave what they had and took what they didn't have.

2 When people 🔟 goods between them, it wasn't possible to know exactly how much things cost.

3 Metal coins in 🔟 had a picture stamped on them.

4 The first 🔟 were made in Sweden.

5 When you travel abroad, you change your money into the other country's 🔟 .

16 Complete the table with information from 14.

History of Money Timeline		
when	**what**	**where**
10,000 years ago	1 🔟	different places around the world
2 🔟	cowrie shells	3 🔟
4 🔟	5 🔟	China, Greece, India
6 🔟	paper money	7 🔟
8 🔟	9 🔟	Sweden

17 Look at the table. It shows the average cost of things in the UK in 1955. Discuss with a partner how much you think the same things cost now. Check the answers at the bottom of the page.

	1955	Now
House	£2,000	🔟
Car	£410	🔟
Cinema ticket	8p	🔟
Pair of shoes	£2.50	🔟
Loaf of bread	5p	🔟
Normal bike	£18	🔟

I think a pair of shoes costs about £50 now.

Yes, I think so, too.

Now: House £163,000   Car £16,495   Cinema ticket £6.53   Pair of shoes £56.42   Loaf of bread £1.02   Normal bike £242.00

Grammar

18 Look, listen and read. Which bag does Belinda want, the red one or the blue one?

Belinda is shopping for a bag.

Shop assistant: Hello, can I help you?

Belinda: Yes, please. I'm looking for a light blue bag. My mum bought it from your shop two months ago. It looked like the red and white ones in the window. Only in blue, of course...

Shop assistant: Do you mean this one?

Belinda: Yes! That's it! That's the one! How much is it?

Shop assistant: It's €49.90.

Belinda: I'll take it.

Shop assistant: Would you like it gift wrapped?

Belinda: No, thanks, but... could you make it look less... new?

Shop assistant: I'm afraid I don't understand.

Belinda: Well, you see, I borrowed my mum's bag without asking her but I lost it. I want to replace it before she finds out. This one is exactly like it, only it looks brand new!

19 Read and complete.

one/ones
Do you mean this bag?
Do you mean this ¹ 🔲 ?
It looked like the red and white bags in the window.
It looked like the red and white ² 🔲 in the window.

Can I ³ 🔲 you?/Could you help us, please?
We're looking ⁴ 🔲 a light blue bag.
How ⁵ 🔲 is it?
It's €49.50 (forty nine euros and fifty cents).
We ⁶ 🔲 take it./I'll take this one.
⁷ 🔲 you like to try it on?
What size is this?
Do you have a bigger/smaller ⁸ 🔲 ?
Which model is it?
What's it made of?

20 Complete with one/ones.

1 Both cars are the same model. The blue ❓ has leather seats as an extra feature.

2 Your trainers are too shabby. You need to buy new ❓ .

3 My new phone can do a lot more things than the old ❓ .

4 We've got two books by the same author. Which ❓ would you like?

5 Which sunglasses look better on me? The black ❓ or these ❓ ?

6 How much are the earphones? The ❓ next to the mobile case?

21 Work with a partner. Make comparisons. Use one/ones.

1 white mp3 player: €59 – 2GB
black mp3 player: €110 – 6GB

2 flowery dress: €50 – not elegant
black and white dress: €150 – very elegant

3 black boots: trendy – uncomfortable
brown boots: not trendy – very comfortable

The white mp3 player is cheaper than the black one.

Yes, but the black one has more gigabytes than the white one.

22 Put the dialogue in the correct order.

Juana is shopping for shoes.

A They're a size 6. Would you like to try them on?

B I'll get them for you. Here you are.

C No, thanks. I'll take the pink ones.

D Of course, miss. What would you like?

E Could you help me please?

F They're €32,99. We've got them in brown, too.

G Yes, thank you.

H I think they're a little too small for you.

I They fit perfectly! How much are they?

J What size are these shoes?

K I'll take them to the cash register for you.

L Yes, I need one size bigger, I think.

Shop Till You Drop

For those who enjoy shopping, every country can offer a different shopping experience. Let's find out about some of the world's most exciting shopping adventures!

1 ?

The Chatuchak Weekend Market in Bangkok, Thailand, is one of the biggest markets in the world and one of the most famous. The market is huge – it covers more than 35 acres in all. It's got more than 15,000 vendors and about 200,000 people or more visit it every weekend. Here you can find everything your heart desires: from a designer pair of jeans to books, coffee makers or a sweet little puppy!

Because Chatuchak is such a big market, and it's got so much variety, you're most probably going to spend quite a lot of time there. To make your visit as enjoyable as possible, don't forget to wear comfortable shoes and clothes, pack a bottle of water and bring enough cash with you as most vendors don't take credit cards. And don't be too shy to haggle. Everyone does!

23 Do you enjoy shopping? Do you think it's fun and relaxing or does it make you feel anxious? Do you like browsing at market stalls or looking in shop windows? Discuss with a partner.

24 Listen and read. Match the titles A–C to the paragraphs 1–3.

A Everything you need

B The Thai experience

C Excitement in Electric Town

> **CONTENT WORDS**
> browse   experience   features   haggle
> products   user's manual   vendor

25 Look at 24 and say which market the statements are about. Say C (Chatuchak), A (Akihabara) or CM (Camden Market).

1 Make sure you buy the right product for you.

2 Always ask the vendor to lower the price.

3 You won't get wet there.

4 It's only open on Saturdays and Sundays.

5 You'll find all the latest models here.

2 ?

In Tokyo, Japan, one of the most popular places for young people is called Akihabara. Akihabara isn't a shop. It's a whole neighbourhood that's known as 'Electric Town'. Young people come from all over the world to buy the latest electronics, video games, animation, computers and more. If you visit and you want to buy something, make sure you ask for the international model that's got the correct features for use in your country, plus a user's manual in English – it's no fun going home to find everything's in Japanese!

3 ?

It's a rainy morning and you're in London. The sky is grey and you want something interesting to do. Why not head to Camden Market? Although it used to be a weekend market, you'll find lots of vendors during the week, too. Fortunately, the market is largely indoors, so you can browse comfortably. With fine arts, traditional crafts, jewellery, clothes, good food and music, there's something here for everyone!

26 Discuss with a partner. Which of the three markets would you like to visit? What would you buy?

> I would like to visit Electric Town. I would buy video games.

> I would like to visit Camden Market. I would buy clothes and jewellery.

27 Write an online review.

You're writing for a travel information site that gives useful tips to tourists visiting your country. Write about a popular market, area, shopping centre or department store in your town. Say where it is and how easy it is to get there. Describe what visitors can do there, what to expect and give a few useful tips.

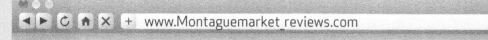

www.Montaguemarket_reviews.com

If you're looking for something to do on a Saturday, then why not head to Montague Market? Situated on the corner of West Street and the High Street, this market is within easy walking distance of the city centre. Whether you're looking for a new pair of jeans, a bite to eat or just a cool place to hang out, Montague Market has got something for everyone!

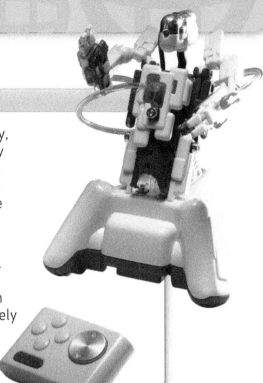

28 Read the product review.

I saved my pocket money for a long time. Then finally, I decided what I wanted to buy. My dad and I bought my remote-controlled robot at Talford's. I brought the box home and opened it. I read the instructions. I put in the batteries. Then I turned the robot on. It made a strange sound and fell over! My new robot didn't work.

So we took it back to the shop and they gave me another robot. I took that one home and it worked fine. I wasn't happy about the first robot but I'm very happy now. This robot is really great. It's more expensive than my other gadgets but it was worth the money. I definitely recommend it.

My Rating ★ ★ ★ ★ ☆

29 Look at the word web. Ask and answer with a partner. Find the answers in 28.

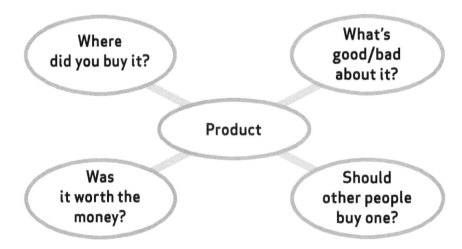

Where did you buy it?

What's good/bad about it?

Product

Was it worth the money?

Should other people buy one?

30 Choose your own product. Copy the word web in 29 into your notebook. In each circle, write answers to the questions. Then use the word web to write your own product review.

31 Share your product reviews with the class. How many good reviews were there? How many bad reviews were there?

32 What do you do with your money? Copy, read and ✔. Then ask a partner.

	always	usually	sometimes	never
1 I spend all my money straight away on things I want.				
2 I like to save my money to buy the things I need.				
3 I use my money to buy presents for other people.				
4 I put my money in a bank. Then I forget about it.				

THINK BIG Do you think you've got good money habits? Why/Why not? Do you think it's important to have good money habits only when you're older? Why/Why not?

PROJECT

33 Design a shopping bag for a shop that helps you spend your money wisely. Be sure to give your shop a name!

34 Work in small groups. Talk about your shopping bags.

Spend Smart Shop

Use our bags and SAVE 10c

We have the lowest prices. If you find something less expensive at another shop, We'll match the price! TO SAVE Use our Smart card to earn a FREE MEAL!

35 Listen, read and repeat.

1 S-C SC   **2** h-o   ho

36 Listen and blend the sounds.

1 m-u-sc-le   muscle   **2** e-c-ho   echo

3 ho-n-e-s-t   honest   **4** sc-ie-n-ce   science

5 g-ho-s-t   ghost   **6** sc-e-ne   scene

37 Listen and chant.

> An honest ghost
> Made an echo
> In our science class.
> Wow! What a crazy scene!

38 Work in pairs. What can you buy or see at a shopping centre? Complete the sentences with your own answers. Then play More or Less.

1 🔑 are delicious.

2 🔑 are expensive.

3 🔑 is an interesting book.

4 🔑 is an exciting film.

5 🔑 is an amazing shop.

6 🔑 is a useful gadget.

Hot dogs are delicious.

Burgers are more delicious than hot dogs.

39 Look, copy and complete. Use more or less.

JUMBLE SALE

£15

£5

1 Wheels

£8

£3

2 Gadgets

£7.50

£12

3 Clothing

£18

£10

4 Jewellery

1 The bike is ? expensive ? the skateboard.

2 The mobile phone is ? the game.

3 The jeans are ? the jacket.

4 The watch is ? the necklace.

40 Look at 39. Role play with a partner.

Hello, can I help you?

Yes please. I'm looking for a skateboard.

I Can

• talk about shopping.

• make comparisons.

unit 5

HOLIDAY TIME

75

1 Read and complete these fun facts about holidays. Use words from the box. Then listen and check.

> kayak   mobile phones   mosquitoes   sunburnt

1 Lost and Found

In 2011, more people lost their ? than their sunglasses while they were travelling!

2 Ouch!

Every year, ? make 700 million people ill!

3 Cover up!

Be careful! You can get ? on a cloudy day if you don't wear sunscreen!

4 Why not fly?

In 2010, a British woman took the longest ? trip that anyone has ever taken – more than 3,200 kilometres!

2

Match. Then listen and check.

1 insect repellent
2 a helmet
3 a warm jacket
4 an anorak
5 a life jacket
6 water bottle
7 a map
8 sunscreen
9 sunglasses

 a
 b
 c
 d
 e
 f
 g
 h
 i

3

Look at the words in the word box. Choose three activities you like. Why do you like them?

Activity	Reason

biking
camping
hiking
horse riding
kayaking
rafting
skiing
swimming

4

Work with a partner. Ask and answer.

What happened when she was hiking?

She got thirsty.

THINK BIG What are the five most important things you should take with you when hiking?

77

5 Listen and read. Why did Jenny enjoy the weekend?

The BEST WEEKEND EVER

by Alison Green

Jenny and her mother were getting ready for a camping trip. Mum was packing their food when Jenny walked into the kitchen.

"Can't we stay at home?" Jenny asked. "I really don't want to go camping," she said.

"But camping is so much fun!" said Mum.

"Sleeping in a tent?" said Jenny. "No TV? That's fun?"

"Yes, it is. We can go hiking! We can make a fire! We can cook sausages outside!" said Mum.

Jenny and her mother arrived at the campsite. They took everything out of the car. Jenny looked up at the sky.

"It's getting cloudy," said Jenny. Suddenly they heard thunder. KABOOM!

"Oh, no!" said Mum. "Let's set up the tent!"

Jenny and Mum were setting up the tent when it started to rain.

"Quick! Get inside the tent!" said Mum.

Jenny waited inside the tent. In a few minutes, Mum came inside, too. Her hair was wet. Her clothes were wet. Her shoes were wet. Everything was wet.

Jenny played her video game while her mother made jam sandwiches. They ate them inside the tent.

It rained all night. And it rained the next day. It rained the whole weekend! Jenny and her mum sat inside. They couldn't go hiking. They couldn't make a fire. They couldn't cook any sausages outside.

After two days of rain, Jenny's mother said, "Time to go home. Please help me take down the tent, Jenny," she said. "Then wait in the car." Jenny waited inside the car with her video game. While Jenny's mother was packing everything into the car, it stopped raining. Then the sun came out. "Now it's sunny," Mum said. She got into the car and started driving home.

Mum said, "You were right, Jenny. That wasn't much fun."

"What? I had a great time, Mum!" said Jenny. "I ate jam sandwiches all weekend and I reached Level 12 on my video game. It was the best weekend ever!"

READING COMPREHENSION

6 Choose the correct answers.

1 When Jenny was looking at the sky, what did she hear?
  a She heard thunder.
  b She heard rain.

3 What did Jenny and her mum eat?
  a They ate sausages.
  b They ate jam sandwiches.

5 When did it stop raining?
  a While Jenny's mum was packing everything into the car.
  b While they were driving home.

2 Why didn't Jenny and her mum go hiking?
  a Because it rained all weekend.
  b Because Jenny was playing her video game.

4 What was Jenny doing while her mum was packing the car to go home?
  a She was making a fire.
  b She was waiting in the car.

6 What did Jenny think about the camping trip?
  a She hated it.
  b She loved it.

THINK BIG Do you think Jenny would like to go camping again? Why/Why not?
Do you like camping? Why/Why not?

Language in Action

79

7 Listen and read. Why was this Daniel's best holiday ever?

Louise: Hi, Uncle Daniel. It's Louise. How was your holiday?

Daniel: Hi, Louise. It was great. It was the best holiday ever!

Louise: Oh, really? What did you do?

Daniel: Well, the first day, I went to the beach. While I was lying on the sand, I fell asleep and woke up with terrible sunburn.

Louise: Oh, no. Really?

Daniel: Yes, so the next day I went hiking in the forest. While I was hiking, I got dozens of mosquito bites.

Louise: Oh, no!

Daniel: Yes. And so the next day I went horse riding. While I was riding, the horse got scared and jumped. I fell off the horse and broke my leg.

Louise: Oh, that's awful! But Uncle Daniel, I'm confused. So why was this the best holiday ever?

Daniel: The doctor says I need to stay at home for a week. I can finally rest and relax!

8 Practise the dialogue in 7 with a partner.

80

9 What happened on Gina's holiday? Listen and match. Then complete the sentences. Use the correct form of the verb.

eat   read   shop   try to sleep

1 She 🔲 when it happened.

2 She 🔲 when it happened.

3 She 🔲 when it happened.

4 She 🔲 when it happened.

| What **was** he **doing** when he got hurt? | He **was riding** a horse when he got hurt. |
| What happened while they **were hiking**? | They got lost while they **were hiking**. |

10 Complete the sentences with the correct form of the verb in brackets.

1 Samuel 🔑 when he got thirsty. (hike)

2 They were kayaking when it 🔑 to thunder. (start)

3 They 🔑 for the bus when it started to rain. (wait)

4 I 🔑 my bracelet while I was swimming. (lose)

5 Alicia broke her leg while she 🔑 . (ski)

6 He 🔑 when he fell in the road. (skateboard)

7 We 🔑 life jackets when we fell in the sea. (wear)

8 Jeremy 🔑 the sausages while he was cooking dinner. (burn)

| **Was** he **riding his bike** when it started to rain? | Yes, he **was**./No, he **wasn't**. |
| **Were** you **swimming** when you got sunburnt? | Yes, I **was**./No, I **wasn't**. |

11 Make questions.

1 (when/Tim/Was/hiking) 🔑 his sunglasses broke?

2 (Billy and Lisa/biking/Were/when) 🔑 they suddenly heard thunder?

3 (shopping/Dan/when/Was) 🔑 he lost his mobile phone?

4 (when/you/Were/horse riding) 🔑 you got stung by the bee?

5 (Were/the hotel/his parents/when/checking into) 🔑 the lights went out?

6 (Sarah/camping/when/Was) 🔑 she broke her arm?

12 Work in groups. How good are you at doing calculations without a calculator, pen or paper? Use your brain only! Who's the fastest?

1 $36 + 5 + 9 = ?$ **2** $89 + 23 + 2 = ?$ **3** $4 \times 12 = ?$ **4** $3 \times 25 = ?$

82

13 Listen and read. What happened to the backpack?

> **CONTENT WORDS**
> addition   customer   item   multiplication
> power cut   price list   receipt   serve   souvenir

First Day at Work!

You've just started a summer job in the shop at Greenfell Mountain National Park. Besides souvenirs, the shop sells items that hikers often need. Unfortunately, while you were serving your first customer, there was a power cut. You can't stop serving your customers. You have to do the additions and multiplications yourself and write them down in a notebook so that customers can come back for their receipts when the power is back on. Here's a short price list:

sunscreen €6.99	disposable camera €9.99	crisps €1.09
insect repellent €5.49	map of the park €2.50	apple 75¢
sunglasses €12.99	bottle of water €1.25	postcards 90¢

Mr Briggs: "Hello. This is my first time hiking and I need some suggestions for what to get. Oh, never mind. I see you've put up a list of suggestions. Perfect! Let's see… insect repellent, sunscreen, two bottles of water and a map. I think that's all. I needn't buy anything else. Wait. I'll have an apple and a bag of crisps, too. How much is it?"

Miss Lee: "Hi. I'm so glad this shop is here. While we were driving here, I realised I didn't have any insect repellent. Can I get three bottles of that, please? Oh, and I forgot to bring a snack for my Year 5 pupils. So I need 15 apples, too. How much is that?"

Amanda: "Oh, hi. Listen. You won't believe what happened to me! I was out hiking this morning when I saw this beautiful flower. I tried to take a picture of it. But while I was opening my backpack, I heard an animal sound and dropped it. My backpack fell down the side of the mountain! Grr! One disposable camera, please. I'm going to try again. Oh, and I need to buy a bottle of water and a pair of sunglasses, too. Everything was in that bag! So, how much is it altogether?"

THINK BIG Do you buy souvenirs from the places you visit? Why/Why not?

14 Look at 13. Read and say true or false.

1 The shop sells souvenirs only.

2 You didn't have time to serve any customers before the power cut.

3 You have to post the receipts to the customers.

4 Mr Briggs is an experienced hiker.

5 Miss Lee needs a bottle of insect repellent for each child in her class.

6 Amanda dropped her backpack when she heard a noise.

15 Work in groups. Ask and answer. Take notes.

You've got a few personal items that you don't want anymore. Why don't you hold a class flea market and sell them? You can use the money to buy other things you like!

1 Make a list of the things you'd like to sell and write the price you're hoping to get for them (be realistic).

2 Exchange lists with other members of your group.

3 Take it in turns to be the buyer and the seller.

4 Ask questions about the things you're interested in and try to get them for a lower price.

5 Take notes of the items you sell and how much you sell them for.

How old is the mp3 player?

I got it for my 8th birthday so it's about 5 years old.

What colour is it?

Black and silver.

I'll give you €10 for it.

That's too little! It cost €90 when it was new!

Yes, but it's old now. I'll give you €25. Deal?

OK, deal!

16 Do your accounts.

Make a list of the items you sold. Add up the money you made. Write the total.
Make a list of the items you bought. Add up the money you paid. Write the total.
Did you make any money or did you spend some of your own, too?

17 **Look, listen and read. Who was Mike meeting?**

Sarah and Mike are having a conversation at school.

Sarah: Where were you going when I saw you yesterday?

Mike: Mmm. What time did you see me? And which direction was I walking in?

Sarah: I think you were walking toward the park and it was about six o'clock.

Mike: Aah, yes!

Sarah: Who were you meeting?

Mike: I was meeting my scout group.

Sarah: But why were you wearing such a warm jacket?

Mike: Well, it gets quite cold in the evenings, you know.

Sarah: Maybe in winter, but not in the middle of summer!

18 **Complete the table with words from the box.**

I   six o'clock   shop   they   was   What

a ¹			**doing** at ² ?
b Why			**singing** loudly?
c Who	**were**	you/we/³	**meeting** last night?
d Which ⁴	⁵	⁶ /he/she/it	**looking** in?
e Where			**flying** to?
f When			**doing** the cooking?

19 **Match each of the questions in 18 to an answer.**

1 I was meeting my cousin Jamie.

2 She was flying to Rio de Janeiro for the carnival.

3 It was looking in the pet shop.

4 Because he wanted everybody to hear him!

5 We were packing suitcases for our holiday.

6 He was doing it at ten o'clock last night.

20 Choose the correct question word and use was or were.

1 A: What/Who ? you watching at 7 p.m.?
B: The news.

2 A: Who/When ? helping you pack your suitcase?
B: Erol.

3 A: Which/Why bus ? Anna and Layla waiting for when we saw them?
B: The 218 for the city centre.

4 A: Why/Where ? Katie crying?
B: She lost her mobile phone.

21 Complete the dialogue.

Fact or Fake???

Canadian hikers have posted a video on YouTube. Apparently, they were hiking when they saw a large creature that looked like Bigfoot or Sasquatch. We interviewed them.

A: ¹ ? (where/you/hike) when you saw the creature?

B: We were in the Tantalus Mountains at about 2000 metres.

A: ² ? (what/it/do) when you started filming?

B: It was climbing a mountain really fast.

A: ³ ? (how fast/it/go)?

B: Really fast, much faster than any human.

A: ⁴ ? (which direction/it/travel) in?

B: Well, it was moving back up the mountain and it was getting dark.

A: You said you were at 2000 metres and the mountain looks very cold and icy.
⁵ ? (why/you/wear) T-shirts?

B: We weren't feeling cold!

A: Mmm, interesting! And ⁶ ? (when/your group/walk) in the Tantalus mountains?

B: In the summer of 2011.

22 Some hikers in Bulgaria say they saw a two-metre-tall alien. Work with a partner. Imagine you're interviewing them. Ask and answer.

Where were you hiking when you saw the alien?

We were hiking in the forest.

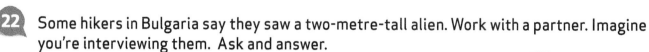

Unique Holiday Destinations

The Museum of Bad Art

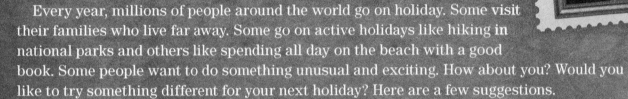

1   Every year, millions of people around the world go on holiday. Some visit their families who live far away. Some go on active holidays like hiking in national parks and others like spending all day on the beach with a good book. Some people want to do something unusual and exciting. How about you? Would you like to try something different for your next holiday? Here are a few suggestions.

2   Try looking at some bad art! The Museum of Bad Art (MOBA), near Boston, Massachusetts, USA, has got more than 600 pieces of the world's worst art. But is the art really that bad? Well, it's enough to say that its founder, Scott Wilson, had the idea when he found a particularly bad painting in a rubbish bin!

3   Put on your warmest coat (we really mean it – a very warm coat) and head over to Ilulissat, Greenland. From there, you can go on an expedition into frozen lands where Arctic foxes, polar bears and other amazing animals live. Where else would you have the chance to stay overnight in an igloo?

Igloo Village

23 What type of holiday do you usually go on? What type of holiday would you ideally like to go on? Discuss with a partner.

85

24 Listen and read. What did Scott Wilson do?

> **CONTENT WORDS**
> arctic   expedition   fascinating   founder   frozen   guide
> guided tour   head over   igloo   particularly   poison   poisonous

25 Look at 24. Correct the mistakes. Write new sentences.

1 The founder of MOBA painted the first painting himself.

2 You can spend the night in a luxury hotel during your expedition to frozen lands.

3 You can't touch the plants in the Poison Garden but it's OK to smell them.

4 People stay away from the beach that's near the airport on St Maarten.

26 Look at 24. Choose one place you want to go and one you don't. Write two reasons for each choice in your notebook.

4   The Alnwick Garden in Northumberland, UK, has got beautiful flowers and plants but, if you visit, remember it's also home to the Poison Garden. Yes, as the name suggests, it's full of poisonous plants! Pay close attention to the signs that say, "Do not touch the plants. Do not even smell them!" But don't be afraid. If you take the guided tour of the garden, the guides will tell you everything you need to know about these dangerous but fascinating plants.

5   St. Maarten in the Caribbean is a beautiful place to spend your holiday if you don't scare easily. Why? Its airport is close to the beach. Too close! Every year, thousands of people stand on Maho beach and wait for planes. The planes fly right over their heads. It's the closest that you and a plane will ever get unless you're on one! And, by the way, when you're on a plane that's about to land on the island, just don't look out of the window!

The Alnwick Garden

Maho Beach

27 What interesting places can you visit in your country? Think of one. Answer the questions in your notebook.

What is it?
Where is it?
What can you do there?
What's unusual or interesting about it?
Why do you like going there?

28 Now write a short description of the place you wrote about.

> Monkey Mount is an adventure playground. You can do activities in the trees. There are zipwires, climbing walls and treetop walkways. It's very exciting because you're high up in the trees but it's also safe. I love going there because it's fun doing these activities with friends.

29 Read Helen's postcard.

date ⟶ 22 February

greeting ⟶ Dear Heather,

    I'm having a great time with my family here at Playa del Carmen! The food at our hotel is great. There are many fun things to do on the beach. But yesterday I got sunburnt while I was playing on the beach. I wasn't wearing enough sunscreen! 🙁 See you soon!

body

closing ⟶ Your friend,
    Helen

Heather Dickinson
31 Church Road
West Hampstead
London
NW3 4PH
UNITED KINGDOM

30 Read the Writing Steps and write a postcard to a friend about your holiday.

1 Think of a holiday place.

2 Write a date and greeting.

3 Write about where you are.

4 Write about why you like it or don't like it.

5 Write about a problem on your holiday.

6 Write a final sentence.

7 Write a closing and sign the postcard.

8 Write an address.

THINK BIG Why do you think people write postcards when they're on holiday? Do you?

31 Work in pairs and discuss. Where do you like to go on holiday? Copy the chart into your notebook and list the kinds of places. Then take turns writing safety tips.

Holiday Place	Pupil 1 Tip	Pupil 2 Tip
The beach	Don't swim straight after eating.	
The mountains		

PROJECT

32 Work with another pair. In your group, make a poster about one of your holiday places. Include your safety tips. Add pictures. Share your poster with the class.

SAFETY TIPS
for the Amusement Park

1 Always wear sunscreen.

2 Take along a water bottle. Drink water often.

3 Know how to contact your parents.

4 Decide on a time and place to meet.

5 Hold onto your camera and other important items.

6 Don't talk to strangers.

33 Listen, read and repeat.

1 c-l   cl   **2** t-w   tw

 34 Listen and blend the sounds.

1 cl-ow-n	clown	**2** tw-i-n	twin
3 tw-i-s-t	twist	**4** cl-o-ck	clock
5 tw-e-l-ve	twelve	**6** cl-a-p	clap

 35 Listen and chant.

> It's twelve o'clock. Time to twist.
> It's twelve o'clock. Time to clap.
> Twist, twist, twist! Clap, clap, clap!

36 Play the Crazy Holiday game. First, choose a word or phrase in each numbered row. Then copy the dialogue and complete it with your choices. Take turns practising the dialogue with different partners.

1	far away	clean	romantic	dirty
2	skiing	drawing	cycling	bird-watching
3	best	worst	most boring	most exciting
4	delicious	old	expensive	spicy
5	Antarctica	the Himalayas	Easter Island	the Sahara Desert
6	get hot	rain	snow	get windy

Ted:	I just got back from holiday.
Joanna:	Really? How was it?
Ted:	It was the ³ ? holiday ever.
Joanna:	Wow. Where did you go?
Ted:	I went to ⁵ ?.
Joanna:	That sounds great.
Ted:	Yes. The food was ⁴ ? and the hotel was ¹ ?.
Joanna:	Wow. That sounds really nice.
Ted:	Uh-huh. But I had some problems, too. While I was ² ?, it started to ⁶ ?.
Joanna:	Oh, no! That's terrible.
Ted:	Yes, but it turned out OK. I'm happy to be home now.
Joanna:	Great. I can't wait to see your holiday photos!

37 Copy and complete the chart. Some words can be used more than once.

> a helmet   a life jacket   a map   a water bottle
> an anorak   insect repellent   sunscreen   walking shoes

What should you take along when you go…

kayaking?	hiking?	biking?

38 Complete the email.

> hiking   mosquito bites   sunburnt   swimming

Hi, Grandma!

We're all having a great time at the beach. Except for Dad. He isn't having a great time. While he was ^{1}? yesterday, he got ^{2}?. He forgot his sunscreen! And Mum isn't having a great time either. While she was ^{3}? in the woods, she got a lot of ^{4}?. She forgot her insect repellent. But now we're in the hotel. We're going to order pizza! See you soon.

Love,
Paul

39 Match the questions and answers.

1 What were you doing when it started to rain?

2 Were you wearing sunscreen when the sun came out?

3 When was Ed riding the horse?

4 Where was Sandra when the mosquitoes bit her?

a In the garden.

b I was hiking in the woods.

c Yesterday morning.

d Yes, we were.

I Can

- talk about holiday problems.

- ask and answer about what was going on when something happened.

unit 6
THE FUTURE!

90

1 Read about these inventions. Are they real or not real? Then listen and check.

1 KEYBOARD JEANS

Keyboard jeans are the latest fashion trend. These jeans come with built-in speakers, a wireless mouse and a keyboard built into the legs of the trousers. This gives new meaning to the term 'laptop' computer!

2 SPRAY-ON BATTERY

The battery in a mobile device can take up almost half of the space in your mobile phone, smartphone or tablet. But now there's a spray-on battery! This battery will be 'painted' onto your mobile device, taking up no room at all.

3 COMPUTER EYEGLASSES

With these computer glasses, you'll be able to do everything you do on a normal computer. There's one big difference: You won't have to carry anything! The lenses are a see-through computer monitor.

4 PET TRAINING APP

Tired of trying to stop your dog from barking in the house? Well, now there's an app for that! This new app for smartphones will stop your dog barking at the touch of a button. It uses special sounds that only dogs understand. You just have to make sure your dog is listening!

2 Listen and find. Which electronic device is the girl talking about?
Then match to the correct words and phrases from the box.

a

b

c

d

laptop computer
mp3 player
smartphone
tablet

3 Listen again. Will we have these devices ten years from now?
Copy and make two lists. Can you add any of your own ideas?

In ten years, we will still have them.	In ten years, we probably won't have them.

4 Work in small groups. Ask and answer.

Will people still use mobile phones ten years from now?

Yes, they will. People will always use mobile phones.

No, they won't. People will find easier ways to communicate.

THINK BIG In ten years' time, what will be the biggest changes at school?
In ten years' time, what will be the biggest changes at home?

5 Listen and read. What happened to the flowers on Rozul?

The Visitor

by Bryan Valverde

When the spaceship landed, the boy was hiding behind the trees. It was a beautiful clear morning. The sun was shining. The birds were singing. The boy just watched the spaceship and waited.

While the boy was watching and waiting, a tall creature suddenly came out of the spaceship. The creature was wearing a silver suit and a large helmet. He started collecting flowers. One by one, he scanned each flower with some kind of camera. Then he typed some information about the flower onto a tablet. When he was finished, he put the flower into a large box.

The creature thought he saw something move and asked, "Is anybody there?" The boy didn't answer.

The creature looked over his shoulder and saw the boy hiding behind the trees. "Oh, there is someone. Hello!" the creature said, "It's all right. You can come closer."

"What are you doing?" the boy asked.

"I'm collecting samples… of flowers," the creature replied.

"Flowers? For what?" asked the boy.

"I'm going to take them back to my planet," said the creature.

"Haven't you got any flowers on your planet?" asked the boy.

The creature sighed. "No, our planet dried up a long time ago. We created too much pollution, we cut down too many trees and now it's like a desert. There's almost no water any more. All of the flowers and trees that lived on our planet are gone."

"That's terrible," said the boy. "Is anyone doing anything about it?"

"Yes. That's why we're collecting samples of life from other planets. Our scientists are working very hard to create water. We use these samples to learn about water. I believe someday, water will return to our planet."

"Wow," the boy said. "What's the name of your planet?"

"It's called Rozul," the creature said. "Long ago, it was very beautiful. If we work hard, someday Rozul will be beautiful again." And then the creature returned to his ship. The boy waved goodbye as the spaceship slowly went up into the air and disappeared.

READING COMPREHENSION

6 Read and say true or false.

1 The boy lives on Rozul.

2 The creature finds out that someone is hiding.

3 There's water on the boy's planet.

4 The creature is collecting samples of flowers.

5 Scientists on the creature's planet are trying to create plants.

THINK BIG Do you think the Earth will always have enough water? Why/Why not? What one thing can everyone do to save water? What can you do to save water on our planet? Name at least two things.

7 Listen and read. How will Ellie get to school today?

Dad: Listen to this. Somebody has invented a flying suit. Can you believe it?

Ellie: Yes, I've heard about it. I want one!

Dad: Start saving your money. This one costs €75,000!

Ellie: Wow. That is expensive! But it won't be expensive in the future. Someday, everybody will have one.

Dad: You're probably right.

Ellie: We'll simply put on flying suits and fly wherever we want. No more planes or airports!

Dad: OK. But today – no flying suits for you! You're going to go on the bus. And you'd better hurry up!

8 Practise the dialogue in 7 with a partner.

9 Listen and match. Then write. Use a word or phrase from the box.

> computer navigation system   smartphone
> tablet   video messaging

| **1** We'll use ❓ to talk to our friends. | **2** We'll use our ❓ to pay for things. | **3** We'll use a ❓ to attend school virtually. | **4** We'll use a ❓ to tell our cars where we want to go. |

| Do you think we'**ll have** cars 100 years from now? | Yes, we **will**. But cars **won't have** drivers! They'**ll use** computers. |
| | No, we **won't**. We'**ll have** spaceships. |

 10 Make predictions about the future. Use won't and will.

1 write letters/send emails

2 buy things in shops/shop online

3 use telephones/use video chatting

4 attend school/use virtual classrooms

5 play with dolls/play with robots

Who will use video messaging in the future?	**Anyone** with a computer and internet access will use video messaging.
Who will send letters to communicate with friends in the future?	**No one/Nobody** will send letters to communicate with friends.
	Everyone/Everybody will use email.
	Well, **someone** might write a letter!

11 Make predictions about the future. Use no one, someone or everyone with will or might.

1 Who will use tablets instead of desktop computers?

2 Who will use a smartphone 100 years from now?

3 Who will use driverless cars?

4 Who will watch DVDs?

5 Who will go to virtual shopping centres?

12 Work with a partner. Guess and write in your notebook three things that robots could do in the future.

13 Listen and read. What types of jobs do robots do? Check your guesses in 12.

> **CONTENT WORDS**
> assistive   capabilities   complicated
> gestures   procedures   repetitive   robotic
> socially   special needs   surgical

Robots: The Present, Not Just the Future

1   What's the first thing that comes to mind when you think about robots?

2   Is it Wall-E, the Disney robot? He was designed to collect rubbish but he accidentally ended up saving the planet. Or do you think of the lovable robots from the Star Wars films, C-3P0 and R2D2? C-3P0 was designed to help humans understand languages and R2D2 could fix anything. Unfortunately, robots with these capabilities exist only in films.

3   However, it probably won't be as far into the future as Star Wars before robots like these exist in real life. Robotic technology has made enormous progress and there are more than a million robots doing all kinds of work for us already. For example, they do boring and repetitive factory work or housework, as well as very dirty jobs. But, more importantly, they do the jobs nobody can do.

4   The Mars rover Sojourner and the underwater robot Caribou are exploratory robots. They help us learn about places that are too difficult or dangerous for anyone to go. But there's also amazing robot technology that can help save lives. The snakebot, for example, is long and thin and can move almost like a real snake. It can move forwards, sideways and even upwards so it can go where no one else can. That means they might be able to find someone trapped in a building after an earthquake or a fire. In the near future, doctors will probably use tiny snakebots for very difficult surgical procedures.

5   The main difference between the robots in films and today's robots is that robots in films actually think. But this, too, will change. Robots have already started doing more complicated tasks. For example, robots have already taught over two million British primary school children about recycling. The next step is socially assistive robots. They can talk and make gestures. The makers of these robots hope that one day they'll help people with special needs.

6   Will a robot best friend be better than a real friend? One good thing about a robot is that it never gets tired or angry. So it'll always be there to help.

THINK BIG Why do you think robots will be helpful for difficult surgical procedures?

14 Look at 13. Read and choose the correct answer.

1 C-3PO was...

   a designed to collect rubbish.

   b good at fixing things.

   c a lovable robot.

2 Robots in films...

   a will never exist.

   b are very popular.

   c will exist sooner than we think.

3 Robots are useful for...

   a expensive and difficult jobs.

   b boring or dangerous jobs.

   c working alone.

4 Snakebots...

   a are used for difficult surgery.

   b could find people.

   c only exist in films.

5 Two million British children...

   a learnt about the environment from a robot.

   b voted for robot teachers.

   c have a robot teacher.

6 The best thing about robots is...

   a they can think.

   b don't get tired or angry.

   c they're cheaper than humans.

15 Look at 13. Copy and complete the table. Can you add any of your own ideas?

Total number of robots working today	Things robots can do now	Things robots will do in the future
	Explore space	

16 Imagine you've got a robot. Decide things you want it to do. Remember these things should make your life easier. Write a description of your robot.

My robot will be small and very friendly. It won't need batteries or electricity. It'll get power from the sun. It'll tidy my room, charge my phone and help me with my homework.

Grammar

17 Look, listen and read. Who will be Leo's English teacher?

Leo is talking to his teacher, Ms Atkins, in the classroom.

Leo: Ms Atkins, will you be our English teacher next year?

Ms Atkins: No, I'm afraid I won't.

Leo: Oh! Will we have classes with Mr Craig instead?

Ms Atkins: No, you won't.

Leo: Oh! Will there be a new English teacher next year?

Ms Atkins: Yes, there will.

Leo: Do you think the new teacher will be as nice as you?

Ms Atkins: Oh, I doubt it. Your new English teacher will be a robot!

18 Read and complete.

	Will	I	**have**	a new teacher?
?	¹ ⏳	you/we/they	**live**	on a different planet?
	Will	he/she/it	**be**	famous?
	Yes,	I/you/he/she/it/we/they	² ⏳ .	
	No,	I/you/he/she/it/we/they	³ ⏳ .	
?	**Will**	there	**be**	a lot of food?
	Yes,	⁴ ⏳	**will**.	
	⁵ ⏳ ,	there	**won't**.	

19 Put the words in order and write the questions in your notebook.

1 watch/will/people/TV/in 100 years/?

2 children/will/go/to/school/?

3 there/will/be/robot surgeons/?

4 everybody/eat/organic/food/will/?

5 will/people/on other planets/live/?

20 What do you think? Ask and answer the questions in 19.

21 Look at these interview questions. Choose the correct questions.

> **1** **a** Do you think everybody will speak English?
> **b** Do you think will everybody speak English?
>
> **2** **a** Will there be really robots that think?
> **b** Will there really be robots that think?
>
> **3** **a** How we will use computers?
> **b** How will we use computers?
>
> **4** **a** Do you think will change the Internet?
> **b** Do you think the Internet will change?
>
> **5** **a** Will people live longer?
> **b** Will live people longer?

22 Complete with the correct words and phrases in brackets.

> **A** In my opinion, ¹ 🔲 be robot nurses, maids, musicians, traffic guards, doctors and lawyers. But ² 🔲 think? No, ³ 🔲 . Researchers have shown that robots can't really think. ⁴ 🔲 just do simple tasks.
> (there will, they won't, they'll, will they)
>
> **B** Well, I think ¹ 🔲 disappear. But ² 🔲 stop using them? No, they ³ 🔲 . However, ⁴ 🔲 computers everywhere, ⁵ 🔲 see them.
> (will people, they'll, won't, we just won't, there will be)
>
> **C** ¹ 🔲 it matter? No, people probably ² 🔲 because ³ 🔲 be pills. ⁴ 🔲 swallow them and know all the languages of the world!
> (will, won't, we'll, there'll)

23 Now match three questions in 21 to the answers in 22. What do you think? Tell a partner.

> I think there'll be robots that will think but they won't think as well as humans.

> In my opinion, there won't be robots that will think. They'll just do simple tasks.

Endangered Languages

1   A language is a living thing. A language needs to be used, otherwise it gets forgotten. There are about 7,000 languages in the world. But roughly every fourteen days, one of these languages is no longer spoken and dies. Experts believe that by 2100, more than half of today's languages will be extinct.

2   There are many reasons why a language starts to disappear. Often it's because the need for the language disappears. Or it can be because fewer and fewer people communicate with it.

3   In Bolivia, more than 30 languages are spoken today. One is a secret language called Kallawaya. The reason it's known as a secret language is because it's only taught by a father to his son or a grandfather to his grandson. Girls almost never learn to speak it. The Kallawaya people use their language for healing and in their family. They don't really use it anywhere else. These days, there are only about twenty people who can speak Kallawaya. With each new generation, fewer males will speak the language and pass it on to their children. Kallawaya is disappearing because of cultural and social changes in people's behaviour.

24 Are there different languages or dialects in your country? Do you know one? Do you think they're important? Discuss with a partner.

102
25 Listen and read. Find three languages or dialects.

> **CONTENT WORDS**
> communicate   dialect   dictionary   extinct   fluently
> generation   healing   official   pass on   preserve

26 Look at 25. Answer the questions.

1 Why is Kallawaya known as a secret language?

2 When and why did the Chinese dialects start disappearing?

3 Why don't Manuel Segovia and Isidro Velazquez talk to each other?

4   Before Mandarin Chinese became the official language of China, there were hundreds of different Chinese dialects. Many of them died out because people stopped using them. Gelo is one of them. The problem is that there are different kinds of Gelo and even some Gelo people can't understand each other. Guo Xiuming still speaks Gelo. She believes she can preserve her language. She's been collecting information about it. She's now got a list of more than 70,000 words. Will she be able to save it? Perhaps, if she creates a Gelo dictionary. But this doesn't mean people will speak the language.

5   There's a language in Mexico that only two people can speak. Manuel Segovia and Isidro Velazquez are the last people who speak Ayapaneco fluently. They live only 500 metres from each other but they refuse to talk to each other. No one knows why. Some people say, "Maybe they just don't have much to say to each other."

27 **Find out about the languages in your country and create a fact file.**

Official language	In the United Kingdom, 95% of the people speak only English.
Number of people who speak it	1 billion people speak English. That's 1 in every 7.
Number of people who learn it	1/4 of the world's population know some or are learning English.
Other languages	Scottish Gaelic, Irish Gaelic and Welsh. 2.7% of the people also speak Bengali, Punjabi, Hindi or Gujaratti.
Number of people who speak those languages	About 59,000 speak Scottish Gaelic, over 1 million speak Irish Gaelic and over 500,000 people speak Welsh.
How useful is your language	English is very useful because many books are in English. 80% of all information stored on computers is in English.

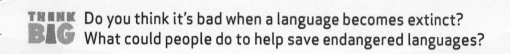

THINK BIG Do you think it's bad when a language becomes extinct? What could people do to help save endangered languages?

28 Read the diary entry.

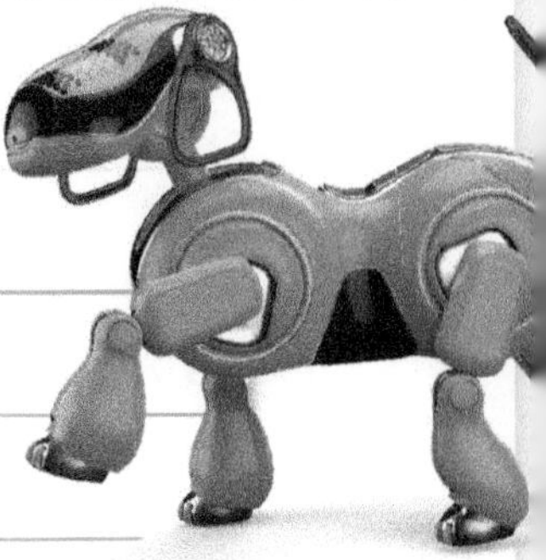

Dear Diary,

I'm exhausted today. After I got home, I had to tidy my room,

do my homework and take the dog for a walk. I can't wait for

the future when we'll have robots to do everything for us. Nobody will ever

complain about doing chores again. We won't have any! Robots will tidy up,

cook and even help us with our homework. So, will I still take my dog for a

walk? Yes, I'll always do that. Everyone needs to get exercise. But one thing

will be different. My dog will be a robot, too!

Good night,

Camilla

29 How does Camilla think her life will be different? Copy and complete the chart.

Now	Future

30 How will your life be different in the future? Write three or four sentences.

31 Use the information in 30 to write your own diary entry. Share it with a partner.

THINK BIG Is it good that life will be different in the future? Why/Why not?

Have dreams for the future. | Life Skills

32 Write four dreams you've got for the future in your notebook. Then compare your dreams with a partner's. Are any of them the same?

1 Someday, I'll

2 Someday,

3 Someday,

4 Someday,

33 Ask and answer with a partner.
1 What's your biggest dream for the future?
2 Why is it important to have dreams for the future?

PROJECT

34 Work in a small group. What kinds of products or services will there be in the future? Design an advertisement. Share your advertisement with the class.

Honey-MOON Hotel
COME AND SPEND YOUR HOLIDAY IN SPACE!

All rooms have a view of the Earth.
Go hiking on the moon
or relax in our space-spa!

35 **104** Listen, read and repeat.

1 p-p pp   2 b-b bb   3 d-d dd

4 m-m mm   5 n-n nn   6 t-t tt

36 **105** Listen and blend the sounds.

1 h-a-pp-y   happy   2 h-o-bb-y   hobby

3 s-u-mm-er   summer   4 l-a-dd-er   ladder

5 t-e-nn-i-s tennis   6 b-u-tt-er   butter

37 **106** Listen and chant.

My favourite hobby
In the summer,
Is playing tennis
And eating bread and butter!

38 Discuss with a partner. Which of the inventions in this picture of The Future do you think we'll have one day? What other inventions do you think we'll have in the future?

The Future

39 Read and complete.

1 In 50 years, who ❓ (use) money to buy things?

Everyone will ❓.

2 In 100 years, who ❓ (drive) cars?

Everybody will ❓.

3 In 100 years, who ❓ (have) robot teachers and virtual classes?

No one will ❓.

4 In 50 years, who ❓ (go) to a cinema to watch a film?

Everyone will ❓.

5 In 100 years, who ❓ (go) on holiday to the moon.

Someone will ❓.

40 Write about two electronic devices that you've got and what you use them for.

41 Write about two electronic devices you think you'll have in the future and what you'll use them for.

42 Answer the questions using anyone, everyone, someone or no one.

1 Who will use video messaging instead of phone calls in the future?

2 Who will use paper and pen to write in 100 years?

3 Who will tidy up their bedroom in the future?

4 Who will read a book in 100 years?

5 Who will ride a bike in the future?

I Can

• ask questions and make predictions about the future.

• talk about technology.

How Well Do I Know It? Can I Use It?

1 Think about it. Read and draw. Practise.

☺ I know this.   😐 I need more practice.   ☹ I don't know this.

	PAGES	☺	😐	☹
Places to shop: mall, craft fair…	59	☺	😐	☹
Things to buy: silver earrings, picture frame…	59	☺	😐	☹
Holiday-related items: map, sunglasses, anorak…	75	☺	😐	☹
Holiday activities: kayaking, camping, hiking…	75	☺	😐	☹
Electronic devices: mp3 player, smartphone, tablet…	91	☺	😐	☹
This camera is **more expensive than** that one. It's **the most expensive** one in the shop. That helmet is **too** small/not big **enough**.	62–63	☺	😐	☹
I like this bag. The **one** with the stripes.	66–67	☺	😐	☹
I lost my ring while I **was swimming**. **Was** he **cycling** when he fell? Yes, he **was**./No, he **wasn't**.	78–79	☺	😐	☹
Why **were** you **singing** loudly?	82–83	☺	😐	☹
We'**ll use** mobile phones 15 years from now. We **won't have** televisions 15 years from now.	94–95	☺	😐	☹
Everyone/Everybody will use email. **No one/Nobody** will use pen and paper.	94–95	☺	😐	☹
Will we **live** on a different planet? Yes, we **will**./No, we **won't**.	98–99	☺	😐	☹

I Can Do It!

2 Get ready.

A Rewrite the dialogue in the correct order. Then listen and check.

Luke: Hey, look at this!

Luke: Well, yes, I suppose that's true. Someone should invent sunglasses that you can't lose.

Luke: Scientists are working on some amazing new sunglasses. Soon, with these glasses, you'll be able to make phone calls, search for things online, take photos and do all kinds of things!

Luke: Really? Why?

Danielle: Because I always lose my sunglasses. I lost some last week while I was hiking. And I guess these amazing new glasses will be more expensive than normal sunglasses.

Danielle: That sounds like a bad idea to me.

Danielle: What?

Danielle: Now that sounds like a better idea!

B Practise the dialogue in **A** with a partner.

C Ask and answer the questions with a partner.

1 What do you think of sunglasses that work like a smartphone? Are they a good idea or not? Explain.

2 Luke describes two kinds of sunglasses. Which kind would you like to have?

3 Do you think technology will make our lives more interesting in the future or more complicated? Explain.

3 Get set.

 STEP 1 Cut out the cards on page 161 of your Activity Book.

 STEP 2 Arrange the cards facedown in two piles: yellow cards and green cards. Now you're ready to **Go!**

4 Go!

A Pick one card from each pile and make up a sentence following the example.

Last weekend while I was camping, I got a lot of mosquito bites.

B Now give advice. What should your partner do differently next time? Then switch roles.

Next time, remember to put on insect repellent!

5 Write about yourself in your notebook.

- What do you think you'll be doing 20 years from now? Where will you be living? What kind of electronic devices will you be using?

- Which holiday sounds more interesting to you, going to the beach or going camping in the mountains? Why?

All About Me   Date:_____

_____

_____

How Well Do I Know It Now?

6 Look at page 106 and your notebook. Draw again.

A   Use a different colour.

B   Read and think.

I can start the next unit.

I can ask my teacher for help and then start the next unit.

I can practise and then start the next unit.

7 Rate this Checkpoint.

very easy   easy   hard   very hard   fun   OK   not fun

1

2

3

4

5

6

7

8

9

Units 4–6 Exam Preparation

 108

Listen and tick the box. There is one example.

What shops did Sally go to today?

 A    B ☐  C ☐

1   What did Sally buy at the shops today?

 A ☐ 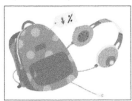 B ☐  C ☐

2   Which tablet is the most expensive?

 A ☐  B ☐  C ☐

3   Which café did Sally have lunch in?

 A ☐  B ☐  C ☐

4   How did Sally come home from the shops?

 A ☐  B ☐  C ☐

5   What is Sally going to take camping?

 A ☐  B ☐  C ☐

Look and read. Write *yes* or *no*.

Examples

No one is wearing shorts.   *no*

There are more than three people swimming in the sea.   *yes*

Questions

1   Five people are kayaking and the tallest person
    who is kayaking is wearing a life jacket.   _____

2   The man who is in the forest is hiking.   _____

3   The woman who's reading her book is wearing
    sunglasses. They aren't big enough for her.   _____

4   All the girls who are lying on the beach have got water bottles.   _____

5   One of the boys who is riding a horse is wearing a helmet.   _____

6   The woman who is walking on the beach and eating an
    apple has got a big yellow bag on her back.   _____

7   The man in the blue hat and brown shorts is talking
    on his mobile phone.   _____

WHAT'S THAT?

109

1

Look at the pictures and read the questions. Choose the correct answers. Then listen and check.

1 What's this used for?
   a giving your hand and wrist a massage
   b playing piano music without a piano
   c typing messages without a keyboard

2 What's this used for?
   a looking for lost items in a pool
   b learning how to swim
   c making phone calls in a pool

3 What's this used for?
   a moving quickly underwater
   b exploring underwater
   c taking pictures underwater

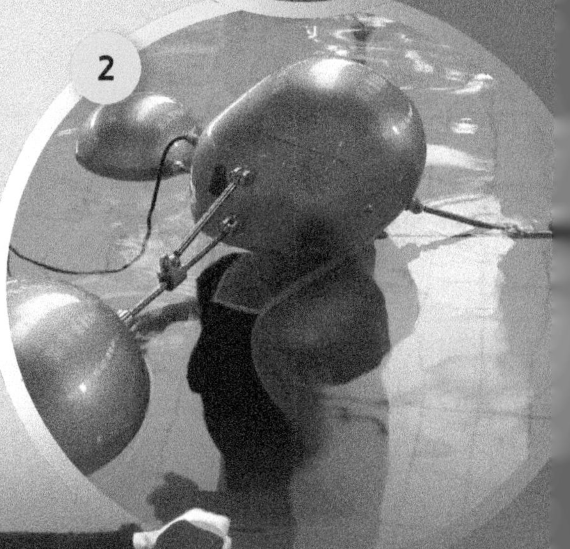

2 Match the gadgets to words or phrases from the box. Then listen and check.

> **a** mobile phone **b** handheld game device **c** hands-free earpiece
> **d** instant camera **e** transistor radio **f** video game system

1  2  3

4  5  6

3 Listen again. Take notes about each gadget and what it was used for.

gadget	what it was used for
instant camera	to take instant photos
	came out in 1948
	was popular in the 70s

4 Work with a partner. Ask and answer. Use your notes from 3.

What is it?

It's an instant camera. It was used to take instant photos. It came out in 1948 and it was popular in the 70s.

THINK BIG Which gadget on this page do you think has changed the most since it was first used? Why?

113

5 Listen and read. What is Mary's necklace worth?

What's It WORTH?

by Lucy Reynolds

CAST

Tim, Mary (brother and sister) | Mr Burns (antiques expert)

SETTING

An indoor antiques market

[Tim and Mary enter the antiques market. They've got a small dish with them. Mr Burns is sitting at a table with some books about antiques on it. There is a sign on the table that says 'Frederick Burns. Antiques Expert'.]

Mary: *[pointing to the dish Tim is holding]* Excuse me, sir. Could you please look at this for us? It might be worth a lot of money.

Mr Burns: *[taking the dish from Tim]* Let's see. What have you got here?

Tim: *[shrugging his shoulders]* I'm not sure. We found it in our attic. It was with our great grandmother's things so it's probably quite old.

Mary: *[running her hand across the dish]* Do you think it was used for sugar or jam?

[Mr Burns picks up the dish and examines it carefully. He doesn't seem to be very impressed.]

Tim: Or maybe to hold jewellery? That's what our aunt Gloria does with her little dish that's just like this one.

Mr Burns: Yes, you're both right about how people use these dishes today. But years ago, this kind of dish was used to hold salt. *[He puts the dish on the table.]*

Mary: Salt?

Mr Burns: Yes. It's probably from the 1930s or so. You see, people used to put salt for each person in these little dishes. After the 1940s, people started to use salt shakers and these little dishes were no longer made.

Tim: So are they worth a lot now?

Mr Burns: No, not really. This one's in pretty good shape. A dish like it was a very common part of a large set of dishes. If you had the whole set – all the plates, saucers, cups and so on – it might be worth a lot. But for just one little dish, I'd say about €6.

Tim: *[disappointed]* I suppose that's why Aunt Gloria just puts her jewellery in it.

Mr Burns: *[Mary reaches over to pick up the dish. Mr Burns suddenly notices the necklace Mary is wearing and gasps in surprise.]* My goodness, where did you get that necklace you're wearing?

Mary: This necklace? It was in a cardboard box with some old costume jewellery that my mother gave me.

Mr Burns: *[in disbelief]* Costume jewellery?

Mary: *[trying to clarify]* You know, it's just fake stuff and cheap. Why?

Mr Burns: *[examining the necklace more closely]* Well, this is a very rare type of necklace from Venice, in Italy.

Tim: Really?

Mr Burns: Yes, indeed. And this particular necklace has got a very unusual design.

Mary: Uh… what's it worth?

Mr Burns: Well, I would say it's worth close to €5,000.

Tim: *[shocked]* Five thousand euros?

[Mary grabs Tim and starts to run away.]

Mr Burns: *[surprised]* Wait! Where are you going?

Mary: *[calling back over her shoulder]* That cardboard box is full of jewellery. I'm going to get it and bring it back here!

END

READING COMPREHENSION

6 Read and say true or false.

1 Tim and Mary are at an art show.

2 They've got a very valuable dish.

3 The necklace isn't just costume jewellery.

4 Mary and Tim leave to bring back more dishes.

THINK BIG Do you think Tim and Mary are glad they took the dish to the antiques market? Why? What makes something that is old, valuable?

7 Listen and read. What is an abacus used for?

Karen:	What in the world is this thing?
Thomas:	I'm not sure. It's one of the weird old things Mr Hartman always brings to class. What do you think it is?
Karen:	It might be a musical instrument. Or maybe it's some kind of old game or toy!
Thomas:	It might be. There's Mr Hartman. Let's ask him.
Mr Hartman:	Oh, hello, you two. What do you think of this abacus?
Thomas:	This what?
Mr Hartman:	Abacus. It's used for adding and subtracting. I'm going to show you how to use it in Maths today.
Karen:	Great!

8 Practise the dialogue in 7 with a partner.

  9 Listen and match. Then complete each sentence with the correct form of a verb or verb phrase from the box.

ice skate	make butter
sleep	warm beds

1 It's used for ❓ . **2** They were used for ❓ . **3** This was used to ❓ . **4** It was used for ❓ .

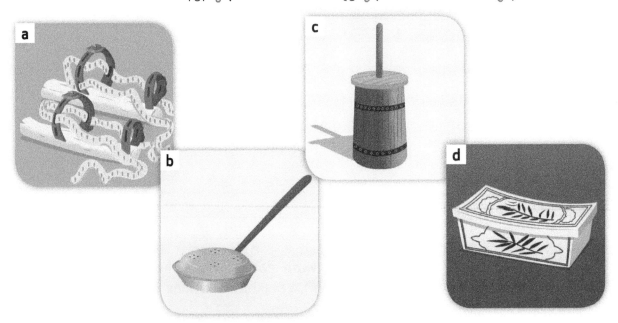

What's it **used for**?	It's **used for** listening to music.
	It's **used to** listen to music.

10 Use words and phrases from the boxes to write sentences with used for or used to.

1 *Pans are used for cooking.*
_____

2 _____

a fork	cook
headphones	eat
glasses	listen to music
pans	read

What is it?	I'm not sure. It **may** be a small plate.
	It **might** be a salt dish.

What **was** it **used for**? Maybe it **was used for** catching fish.

11 Look at the pictures. What do you think these things are? What do you think they were used for? Make sentences using the words and phrases from the boxes.

fish trap	catch fish
ice tongs	cook
pressure cooker	pick up ice

It might be a pressure cooker.

Maybe it was used for cooking.

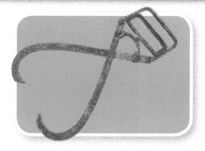

12 Take two minutes. Look around you. What are the most useful items for everyday life that you can see? Write a list in your notebook and compare it with a partner.

118

13 Listen and read. Match each invention a-e to a paragraph 1-5.

a Light Bulbs **b** Computers
c The Wheel **d** Combustion Engine
e Indoor Plumbing

> **CONTENT WORDS**
> candle cash register combustion engine
> fuel invention/inventor organise
> plumbing pump vehicle well wheel

The Greatest Inventions: Your Top Five

There are so many things around us that make life easier. What might life be like without them? We asked our readers what they thought were the most useful inventions from the past. Here are their top five.

1 It all starts here. If you haven't got wheels, you can't go anywhere or get anything! We need them for every type of vehicle. They take us places and bring things fast. They're used for operating many kinds of machines. Wheels were used as far back as 3000 BC.

2 Imagine it's extremely cold or extremely hot. If you want some water, you've got to go to the well or a pump. Or even worse, your toilet is outside. Before indoor plumbing, people had to do this. Try to think about all the times you turn on the water in your home every day. The ancient Greeks invented it nearly 4,000 years ago. Unfortunately, there are still some countries where they haven't got it.

3 Until 1879, candles or oil lamps were used for lighting. But then Thomas Edison developed the bulb. Walk around your home and count how many light bulbs you see. They're everywhere – even inside your fridge!

4 This can get you somewhere far and fast. If there isn't one of these in your car, train or bus, you can't get to the shops or the cinema. Thank the inventor of the combustion engine. In a combustion engine, fuel burns and makes power. The power from the engine is used for making vehicles run. By 1860, people knew how to make combustion engines but they didn't start making lots of them for a few more years.

5 You might use one of these to do your homework, organise your schedule or read a magazine. But computers are also used for running things that you use every day. There are tiny computers inside cars, microwave ovens, cash registers in shops and vending machines. Charles Babbage invented the first computational machine in 1822 but it has changed a lot since then.

These are only the readers' top five. How many more great things can you think of?

 THINK BIG Do you agree with the order of the list? Why/Why not?

14 Look at 13. **Read and complete.**

1 Wheels aren't just for operating vehicles, they're also used for 🔧 .

2 The ancient Greeks had water in their homes 🔧 years ago.

3 The electric light bulb was invented by 🔧 .

4 People could stop using candles in 🔧 .

5 The internal combustion engine works by burning 🔧 .

6 Computers today aren't the same as Charles Babbage's 🔧 from 1822.

15 **Ask and answer questions with your partner to complete your fact files. Guess the inventions.**

Student A

What/the invention?
When/invent?
Who/invent?
What/used for?
How/useful/today?

dPio
2001
Steve Jobs and his team at Apple invented it.
- storing/listening to music
- watching DVDs
✔ very useful
✔ keep a lot of music in one place
✗ now people put music on their phone instead

Student B

tchwawrist
1868
Patek Phillipe – for Countess Koscowicz of Hungary
- a small timepiece
- can wear it on your wrist
- put it in your pocket
- tells the time
✔ they look nice
✔ very useful
✗ now people use their mobile phones or computers instead

What/the invention?
When/invented?
Who/invent?
What/used for?
How/useful/today?

16 **Work with a partner. Think of five more inventions and create your own top ten list of useful inventions.**

My number one invention is electricity because without it so many things at home and at school wouldn't work.

Yes, I agree, and number two is running water because we need water in our homes and schools for many things, too.

17 **Choose an invention from your top ten list and create a fact file for it. Use the fact files in 15 as an example.**

18 Look, listen and read. What happens if you use this candle?

Ian and Selda are talking about an invention.

Ian: Hey, look at this cool invention. If you use this candle, you never need to buy a new one. When you light the candle, it'll make a new one under it.

Selda: But what's it used for?

Ian: Well, you get light when you light a candle.

Selda: What's so special about that? If you've got electricity in your house, you've already got light!

Ian: Yes, but if you haven't got electricity, what do you do?

Selda: If you haven't got electricity, you probably haven't got enough money to buy that candle!

19 Complete the table with words from the box.

cook   if   is   light   when

If/When + present --- present	**If** you ¹ 🔲 a candle, you **get** light.
	² 🔲 it **is** summer in the USA, it ³ 🔲 winter in Australia.
	I **go** to bed early ⁴ 🔲 I **feel** tired.
	We always ⁵ 🔲 at home **if** we **don't go** out for the day.

20 Read and match.

1   When the sun goes down on one side of the world,

2   If you use good sunglasses,

3   People don't like it

4   The sea is very cold

5   You are easy to see

6   If you've got a GPS navigation system,

7   When you use a compass,

8   What do you do

a   if there are ants in your kitchen?

b   you never get lost.

c   they protect your eyes.

d   you know where north is.

e   it comes up on the other.

f   if you behave badly in public.

g   if you swim in it in February.

h   when you wear brightly coloured clothes.

21 Complete the sentences with the correct form of the verbs in brackets.

1 If Felipe 🏵 flippers in the sea, he 🏵 faster. (wear, swim)

2 Mum 🏵 angry when we 🏵 our homework. (get, not do)

3 If the weather 🏵 bad, I 🏵 to school. (be, not cycle)

4 Eli 🏵 a book when he 🏵 the train? (read, catch)

5 We 🏵 to school if it 🏵 a lot. (not go, snow)

6 Our cat 🏵 food if you 🏵 her. (steal, not feed)

22 Make true sentences for you and your family.

1 If I don't tidy my room, 🏵

2 When Dad does the cooking, 🏵

3 If it's a rainy day, 🏵

4 If it's a lovely summer day, 🏵

5 If I want to stay up late, 🏵

6 If I get really good grades at school, 🏵

23 Look at 22. Interview your partner. Compare your answers.

What do your parents do if you don't tidy your room?

Well, if I don't tidy my room, I don't get any pocket money. What about you?

24 Choose the correct answer.

1 If you eat too much or too fast,...

  a you get stomachache.   **b** you got stomachache.

2 In the summer, you get sunburnt if you...

  a don't put on sunscreen.   **b** will put on sunscreen.

3 If Irini sleeps well,...

  a she felt happy.   **b** she feels happy.

4 We always wear raincoats when...

  a it rained.   **b** it rains.

Cool Transformations

1   Designers are very creative people and they make things look attractive. But they're also brilliant at transforming everyday objects. There are talented designers in every country. When they design, they try to think about their country's resources and the problems they can solve. If a design can use resources, solve a problem and have more than one use, then it's really brilliant. Three great designs do just that.

2   Austria is one of Europe's largest suppliers of wood. In Austria, the forests grow an average of 15,000 acres per year. Austrian tree logs are often cut up and used for firewood. They're also used for building furniture or even homes. But one company in Austria used this fantastic natural resource to make large speakers for mp3 players! The mp3 player connects to a dock on the log and the log has got big speakers inside. The clever design company discovered that if you put speakers inside a hollow log, it makes the sound much better.

25 Work with a partner. Match these objects to a use. Which transformation idea is best?

1	tree log	**a**	store earrings and rings
2	ice cube tray	**b**	dog or cat bed
3	an old suitcase	**c**	a seat

26 Listen and read. Which design could save your life?

> **CONTENT WORDS**
> combine   connect   dock   innovative
> natural resource   speakers   supplier   transform

27 Look at 26. Answer the questions.

1 How do the speakers make the music sound?

2 In which room is the Italian aquarium?

3 What material is the shopping bag made of?

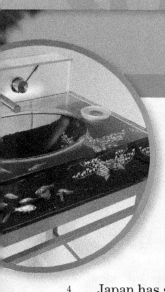

3   In Italy, great design is its greatest resource. One designer combined design with stress relief therapy. Many people find watching fish in an aquarium calming. Some people have got aquariums at home but they're usually in a family room or a living room. However, one clever Italian design company brought an aquarium into the bathroom so they designed an aquarium sink! It's a great way to save space. And what better place for an aquarium than a place where we use water? If you like the sink, the company also sells aquarium toilets!

4   Japan has got many great natural resources but it also suffers from one big problem – earthquakes. What do you do if you're out shopping and there's an earthquake? An inventor in Japan has designed a multipurpose shopping bag that might save your life. If you empty the bag, turn it upside down and put it over your head like a hat, it protects you from falling objects. The bag is made of the same material as construction helmets.

5   Designers all over the world are turning everyday objects into exciting things. Could you make something innovative out of something ordinary?

28 Work with a partner. Look on the Internet for ideas. Then write about great ways to reuse the objects below. Present them to the class.

- An old metal dust bin
- An old bookshelf
- A big glass jar
- An old tea cup and saucer

 THINK BIG Do you think using everyday objects for more than one thing can help the environment? How?

29 Read the paragraph describing an invention.

A Great Invention

This invention is used for finding your way around in the woods or in unfamiliar areas. It's small and round. In fact, it's small enough to fit in your pocket! When you open it, you'll see that it's got a needle. The needle points to the north. This device practically guarantees that you'll never get lost! This important invention is a compass.

30 Copy and complete the second column of the chart with details used to describe the invention in 29. Compare with a partner.

Ways To Describe It	Invention: Compass	My Invention
What it looks like	small, round	
What it's got		
What it's used for		
Why it's important		

31 Write about an invention.

   A Choose an invention. Write notes in the third column of your chart.

   B Use notes from the chart to write a description of your invention. Don't mention its name until the last line.

32 Share your description.

   A Share your description with the class. Don't read the last line. Ask the class to guess your invention.

   B Discuss which inventions you were able to guess and then talk about the new information you learnt.

33 Work in a small group. Copy and complete the chart, using information you know or can find out about England. If you prefer, choose a different country and create your own chart.

ENGLAND

People	Places	Events

34 Exchange charts with another group. In your group, discuss the other group's chart. For people, places and events you don't know, try guessing. Use may and might to narrow your guesses.

PROJECT

35 Create a page for a class book about items that are unique to different cultures.

1 Draw or bring in a picture of an item that is unique to your family's culture.

2 Write what it is, what it's used for and any other information.

3 Put all the pages together to make one book for your class.

Piñata
Used for celebration
Made of paper with sweets inside

This is a piñata. It's used for playing a party game. It's got sweets inside. People wear blindfolds and hit it with a stick. When it breaks open, everyone runs to pick up the sweets!

THINK BIG What cultural item in your class book do you find most interesting? Why?

123

36 Listen, read and repeat.

1 l-t   lt   2 l-k   lk

3 l-d   ld   4 l-b   lb

124

37 Listen and blend the sounds.

1	b-e-lt	belt	**2**	m-i-lk	milk
3	c-o-ld	cold	**4**	b-u-lb	bulb
5	s-i-lk	silk	**6**	f-ie-ld	field

125

38 Listen and chant.

> Lets...
> Drink cold milk,
> Wear a felt belt
> And a silk scarf!
> And put a green bulb
> In the spotlight!

126

39 Work with a partner. What do you think it is? What was it used for? Use may be or might be in complete sentences. Then listen and check.

1

2

3

4

Rewrite the sentences in order to form a conversation.

Kevin: A package? Oh, good. It may be the new game I ordered.

Kevin: Let's see… no, it's too heavy for a computer. Wait. There's a little label here.

Kevin: Well, if it is, it looks like and feels like a lot of dog food!

Alice: Look! There's a package by the door.

Alice: You're right. The label says, 'Canine Power Mix'. Oh, now I remember! I think it might be the new organic dog food for Max!

Alice: No, it can't be a game. The box is too big! It might be the computer Dad ordered.

 Choose one thing. Write three sentences about what it's used for. Then work in small groups and compare your sentences.

  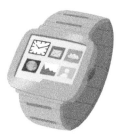

 A (smartphone/computer/watch) is used for…

 Work in small groups. Write quiz questions for other groups. Follow the example.

If you heat water to 100° Celsius, it…

It boils!

Correct! One point.

I Can

- guess what things are or might be.
- say what things are used for or used to do.
- make true sentences using conditionals.

WHERE DO THEY COME FROM?

1 Read and guess where the ideas come from. Write countries from the box. Not all of them will be used. Then listen and check.

Canada China Japan Norway the Philippines the United States

1 Superman, the chocolate nut bar, basketball and even the green rubbish bag were all created in ⟨?⟩.

2 CDs, high-speed passenger trains and the cultured pearl were all created in ⟨?⟩.

3 Three inventions that make food shopping easier – the automatic door, the shopping trolley and the barcode reader – were invented in ⟨?⟩.

4 The world's first karaoke machine was made in ⟨?⟩.

5 What became the first aerosol spray can was developed in ⟨?⟩.

2 Read the list of products. What are they made of? List them. Some can be listed more than once. Then listen and check.

1 These things are made of **cotton**. **2** These things are made of **rubber**.

PRODUCTS

blankets	planes
boots	plates
cola cans	rugs
cookers	scarves
floors	towels
flower pots	T-shirts
jumpers	tyres

3 These things are made of **metal**. **4** These things are made of **wool**. **5** These things are made of **clay**.

3 Listen. Where do the materials come from? Match. Two materials come from the same place. Listen again and check.

1 Rubber comes from   **a** animals like sheep.
2 Metal comes from   **b** the Earth's crust.
3 Cotton comes from   **c** a plant.
4 Wool comes from   **d** a liquid found in trees.
5 Clay comes from

4 Ask and answer.

What material are rugs, towels and T-shirts made of?

They're made of cotton.

THINK BIG What do you think is the most important material? Why?

5 Listen and read. Where was pizza first made?

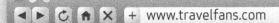

www.travelfans.com

travelbug	Help! My family and I are thinking about going to Italy for a holiday. We've only got five days to spend there so we can't see everything. Where should we go?
castle_hopper	Hi, travelbug. You should definitely come to Tuscany. There's so much to do here and everything is close by. Florence is the capital of Tuscany. It's known for its beautiful palaces, churches and other buildings. Many of the most famous works of Renaissance art can be found here in the museums and galleries. You could spend five days just looking at the art in Florence! Siena is a beautiful medieval town. It's filled with incredible old buildings. If you've got time, go to the Palio de Siena, a medieval horse race that's held twice a year. It's attended by thousands of people, so be prepared!

Florence

Palio de Siena

seat1A_flyer	Hey, travelbug! If this is your first trip to Italy, you should definitely see Rome. This city is known for some of the most famous sites in the world: the Colosseum, the Pantheon, the Spanish Steps… the list goes on and on! Vatican City, the smallest country in the world, is located inside Rome, too. And you can't leave Rome without seeing the ceiling of the Sistine Chapel. The ceiling was painted by Michelangelo and is *amazing*! If you're in Rome, you could easily go on a quick trip down to Naples. It's been called the birthplace of pizza and is located on the beautiful Amalfi Coast. So you can enjoy your pizza while you sit and look out at the sea!

Colosseum

Vatican City

www.travelfans.com

getaway_gary73

Ciao, travelbug. Rome and Tuscany are nice but for something really unique, try Venice. Venice is known around the world as a floating city. Most of its 'streets' are filled with water! They're called canals. To get around Venice, you can take a water taxi.

Some of the most beautiful buildings in the world were built in Venice. There's the Piazza San Marco – a beautiful city square next to St Mark's Cathedral. This site is visited by thousands of people every year. You can find some unique souvenirs here, too. You could get a necklace made of Murano glass. Or you could buy one of those famous masks from the Venice Carnival. The masks are known around the world. They're worn during celebrations at Carnival time here. Venice really is an incredible place.

Venice

Piazza San Marco

READING COMPREHENSION

6 Read and say true or false.

1 Tuscany is the capital of France.

2 The medieval horse race is held twice a month in Siena.

3 The ceiling painted by Michelangelo is located in Rome.

4 Venice is often called the birthplace of pizza.

5 Most streets of Venice are crowded with cars.

6 Murano glass is produced in Venice.

THINK BIG Why do you think Italy is visited by millions of people each year? Which place in Italy would you like to visit? Why?

Language in Action

7 Listen and read. What new information does Sue find out about Costa Rica?

Martin: I can't wait. We're going to Costa Rica next week!

Sue: Costa Rica? I don't know much about that country.

Martin: Well, you've come to the expert! What do you know about it?

Sue: I know that it's in Central America.

Martin: It is! But can you guess what it's known for? A third of the country is made up of them.

Sue: I haven't got a clue.

Martin: Its rainforests! A lot of agricultural products come from there, too. In fact, that banana you're eating was probably grown there.

Sue: This banana? How do you know?

Martin: Read the sticker on it.

Sue: Costa Rica... you're so clever!

8 Practise the dialogue in 7 with a partner.

9 Listen and match. Then complete the labels with words from the box.

> China   Hungary   Morocco   Saudi Arabia

1 Made in 🔖   **2** Made in 🔖   **3** Made in 🔖   **4** Made in 🔖

a

b

c

d

| That watch **is made** in Switzerland. | The first pizza **was** probably **made** in Italy. |
| Those bananas **are grown** in Ecuador. | The first noodles **were** probably **made** in China. |

Tip: To form the passive, use the present simple or past simple form of the verb *be* with the past participle of the main verb.

10 Put the words in order to make statements.

1 Switzerland/in/made/watches/are

2 bananas/in/Ecuador/are/grown

3 was/the/made/pizza/first/Italy/in

4 the/were/noodles/first/China/in/made

5 in/strawberries/grown/are/England

6 first/bar/the/Canada/chocolate/made/was/in

11 Make sentences. Use the present simple passive form of the verb in brackets.

1 Sheep ？   (raise in/China)

2 Diamonds ？   (mine in/Africa)

3 Pottery ？   (make in/Italy)

4 Coffee ？   (export from/Costa Rica)

5 Rubber ？   (produce in/Brazil)

12 Complete the sentences. Use the past simple passive form of the correct verb from the box.

> design   eat   import   sell

1 Millions of mobile phones ？ in Japan last year.

2 This video game ？ in Spain.

3 A lot of pizza ？ in Britain last year.

4 All the flowers in this market ？ from Holland.

13 Work with a partner. Answer the questions about the foods in the box.

1 Are these foods grown in your country? Where do they grow?
2 In which season should they grow?
3 How often or when do you eat them?

apples
grapes
green beans
mangoes
peaches
tomatoes

136
14 Listen and read. How do people eat any food all year round?

> **CONTENT WORDS**
> country of origin diesel distribution centre fresh produce imported
> local locally-grown petrol pollution seasonal shipping typical

From the Farm to Your Plate

1   Imagine you're at a restaurant. You order a salad with beautiful green lettuce, nice red tomatoes, yellow peppers and cucumber. When it comes, you can't wait to take that first bite. But stop for a moment and think about how long it actually took to get to your plate. Not from the kitchen but from the farm.

2   Let's take a look at a typical salad served in the United Kingdom. 'Fresh' food, such as the lettuce, might be grown locally. But what about the other foods on your plate? Nowadays, the country of origin of most of our fresh produce – that's the place where it was grown – is thousands of kilometres away. It was picked, washed, packed and brought to a distribution centre halfway around the world before it travelled to a store near you. So food which looks fresh has actually travelled in a refrigerated van for a week.

3   But that isn't the only problem. Food needs transportation, and all forms of transportation cause air pollution. The farther food travels, the more petrol and diesel fuel are used, the more pollution is released into the air we breathe. Shipping fresh produce can add up to forty-five times more pollution to the air.

4   There is a solution, however. We can stop eating imported foods and buy fresh produce grown locally instead. The lettuce picked yesterday at a local farm will taste a lot better. It'll also be healthier. Eating locally-grown produce also means that you eat more variety. We forget that different fruits and vegetables grow in different seasons. They're seasonal. That means we can't eat fresh summer fruit and vegetables in winter. But we really shouldn't anyway!

5   Do you shop at your local farmers' market or fresh produce stand? You should try it. Next time you order a salad, ask where the produce was grown. You'll be able to tell what's fresh. You'll also get an idea of the pollution it has caused!

THINK BIG Isn't it better to have food you like all year round, no matter how far it travels? Why/Why not?

15 Look at 14. Choose the correct answer.

1 Fresh produce in the UK…

  a has to be grown locally.

  b sometimes comes from far away.

3 It's better to eat local produce than produce from far away because…

  a it contains different vitamins.

  b it causes less pollution.

5 If we eat locally-grown produce,…

  a we eat less variety.

  b we only eat seasonal fruit and vegetables.

2 When the vegetables arrive at the distribution centre,…

  a they are clean.

  b they are put into new bags.

4 Freshly picked vegetables…

  a taste much better.

  b cost less money.

6 We can find local produce when we shop at…

  a farmers' markets or food stands.

  b supermarkets.

16 Copy the chart in your notebook. Use information from 14 to complete the fact file. Compare your answers with a partner.

Imported food facts		Locally-grown food facts	
Advantages	Disadvantages	Advantages	Disadvantages

17 Work with a partner. Ask and answer about the food you like. Use the prompts.

- What are your favourite fruit and vegetables?
- When are most of your favourite fruits in season where you live?

What do you like eating?

Well, I really like melon and strawberries. What about you?

I love grapes. When are they in season where we live?

In the summer. What's in season in winter?

18 Look on the Internet for information about some of the fruit and vegetables from your country. Write in your notebook when they're in season.

138

19 Look, listen and read. Where have the coffee beans been?

There are coffee producers in Indonesia whose coffee is more expensive and better than any other coffee in the world – Kopi Luwak. People who drink this coffee say it's wonderful. However, the place where it's actually made isn't very nice. Kopi Luwak is made from coffee beans which have been inside a civet's stomach! Coffee cherries are fed to the civet. Then the coffee producer waits for the moment when the civet needs the toilet and collects the waste. The Kopi Luwak coffee beans are found in the waste – untouched! The coffee drinkers that choose Kopi Luwak pay about €50 for each cup!

20 Complete the table with words from the box.

that   when   where   which   whose

The person **who**/ ¹❓ answered the phone was my brother.
The coffee ²❓/**that** he bought cost a hundred euros.
That's the lady ³❓ daughter is a coffee producer in Brazil.
The National History Museum is a place ⁴❓ you can see dinosaurs.
January is a period ⁵❓ a lot of stores have sales.

21 Read and choose.

1   The room **when/where** I saw the mouse is near the kitchen.

2   Uncle Marcos has got a friend **who/whose** only drinks Kopi Luwak.

3   We can't wait for the day **that/when** school stops for summer.

4   That's the man **that/whose** dog wears a special coat.

5   Alpaca is wool **who/which** comes from a small South American animal.

6   Is that the student **who/whose** invention won a prize?

22 Read and complete.

1 Venice is the place 🔑 Murano Glass is made.

2 Costa Rica is a country 🔑 is in Central America.

3 You should visit the museum on a day 🔑 everybody is at school.

4 Asya is a girl 🔑 parents are both from Turkey.

5 White water rafting is a sport 🔑 is done on fast rivers.

6 Miranda is someone 🔑 likes wearing pretty clothes.

23 Find the extra word in each sentence. Then say the sentence correctly.

1 Birmingham is the place in the UK where you can see Tower Bridge there.

2 Bottles that they are made of glass can be recycled.

3 A jumper that it is made of cotton is very warm.

4 Michelangelo is the man who he painted the Colosseum.

5 Christopher Columbus is the man whose his boat sailed to the North Pole.

6 An ostrich is a bird which it can't run fast.

24 Are the sentences in 23 true or false? Work with a partner. Use the words from the box as clues.

> New York   Sistine Chapel   the Americas   wool

I don't think Birmingham is the place where you can see Tower Bridge. I think it's London.

I think you're right.

25 Match the sentences. Then link the sentences and write them in your notebook. Cross out any extra words.

1 Wellingtons are rubber boots.

2 Lake Nakuru is a place in Africa.

3 Mr Jenson is a neighbour.

4 A parachute is a large piece of material.

5 Vincent Van Gogh was a brilliant painter.

6 Late autumn is one of the times.

a He became famous after he died.

b The northern lights are strong in Norway.

c You can see thousands of flamingoes there.

d It's used for sky diving.

e His dog is very noisy.

f They're made for wet weather.

Where Did It Really Come From?

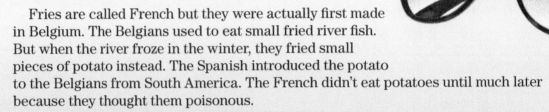

1   Think of spaghetti, and Italy comes to mind. How about French fries? Well you shouldn't think of France because that isn't where they really come from…

2   Fries are called French but they were actually first made in Belgium. The Belgians used to eat small fried river fish. But when the river froze in the winter, they fried small pieces of potato instead. The Spanish introduced the potato to the Belgians from South America. The French didn't eat potatoes until much later because they thought them poisonous.

3   In China, people have been making noodles since 3000 BC. The Italian explorer Marco Polo brought noodles to Europe in the 13ᵗʰ century. This became spaghetti! Thomas Jefferson brought spaghetti to the US from France in the 1700s.

26 Work with a partner. Guess which countries these things come from.

1 fries

2 spaghetti

3 matches

4 fridges

27 Listen and read. Check your answers in 26. Write the countries where each object comes from.

> **CONTENT WORDS**
> borders   chemical   county   engineer   explorer
> novelty   power tools   fridge

28 Complete the sentences with these numbers.

1 The Chinese have been making noodles since ? .

2 Thomas Jefferson visited France in the ? and brought spaghetti to the USA.

3 In ? , John Walker created a match.

4 The first fridge was built in Dublin in ? .

5 In ? , John Spilsbury had the idea for the jigsaw puzzle.

1700s
1767
1894
3000 BC
1827

4   What are the origins of some everyday household objects?

5   The Chinese gave us fireworks but Englishmen invented the match. Robert Boyle found a way to make fire by mixing phosphorus and sulphur. In 1827, John Walker used this chemical combination to create a match. It was one metre long!

6   A German engineer discovered the process of refrigeration. Carl Von Linde discovered that if you combine special gases, they stay cold. He made the first fridges in Dublin, Ireland, in 1894. Fridges today keep our food fresh.

7   What about novelties like sunglasses or jigsaw puzzles? For centuries, Chinese judges wore smoke-coloured glasses. But they weren't for protection; they hid the judges' eyes in court so no one could guess their thoughts. The idea for the jigsaw puzzle came from John Spilsbury in 1767. He was a teacher who wanted to teach his students geography. He glued a map of England and Wales to a flat piece of wood. Then he cut out the map along county borders. After mixing up the pieces, his students made the map puzzle. The jigsaw puzzles which we see today were invented about 100 years later.

8   So are you sure about an object's origins? The label might say one thing but the idea probably came from somewhere else!

29 Ask and answer about these people.

Carl Von Linde   Marco Polo   Robert Boyle   John Walker   John Spilsbury

Who was Carl Von Linde?

He was the man who...

30 Is anything famous produced in your country? What? Think of three products. Were any famous discoveries made in your country? Which ones?

31 Choose one of the inventions or discoveries from 30 or choose one that you find interesting. Create a short list of fun facts and write about it.

Origin	First grown in Peru by Incas in 8000 BC
Discovery	Spanish Conquistadors in 1536
Travel	Went to Ireland with Sir Walter Raleigh
Interesting facts	They contain all the vitamins we need.
Problems	There was a potato blight in the 1840s.

Potatoes were first grown in Peru by the Incas in 8000 BC...

32 Read the paragraph. Find the main opinion. Note down three reasons used to support it. Do the reasons persuade you to visit Corsica? Discuss with a partner.

Come to Sunny Corsica!

main opinion →

This beautiful island paradise, a territory of France, is located in the beautiful Mediterranean. It's made up mostly of mountains, which run from north to south in a single chain. The coast, however, offers vast stretches of fabulous beaches. It's the perfect place for a family holiday! The main languages spoken here are French and English, making it easy to find out everything you need to know. The island is known for its hiking in spectacular mountainous scenery. It's also popular for diving along its unspoilt and wild shoreline. But, if you want a less active holiday, Corsica is also the perfect place for sunning yourself on one of its magnificent beaches. The island's rich history makes it perfect for those wanting culture, too! Come and visit Corsica and find out firsthand why it's known for being a top holiday destination!

33 Choose your favourite holiday spot. Write a topic sentence expressing your main opinion. Write three reasons.

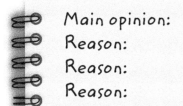

> Main opinion:
> Reason:
> Reason:
> Reason:

34 Use the information you listed in 33 to write a paragraph.

35 Exchange paragraphs with your partner. Did your partner's reasons persuade you?

THINK BIG Why does travel writing try to persuade people?
What other examples of writing that tries to persuade people can you think of?

36 Copy and complete the chart for each category. Follow the examples. Then discuss with a partner.

What I appreciate	Where it comes from
The food I eat *fruit like oranges* *salad*	*right here in Spain* *local markets and right in my garden*
The clothes I wear	
The transport I use	
The technology I use	

37 Work in small groups. Compare your charts. Do you appreciate some of the same things?

> I like my jeans. They're made of cotton from China.

PROJECT

38 Choose a category from the chart in 36. Draw or find pictures to make a poster. Label where each comes from. Give a presentation about your poster.

39 Listen, read and repeat.

1 l-f   lf   2 l-p   lp   3 l-m   lm

 40 Listen and blend the sounds.

1 g-o-lf   golf   2 h-e-lp   help

3 f-i-lm   film   4 e-lf   elf

5 e-lm   elm

 41 Listen and chant.

School clubs are fun clubs!
Golf clubs,
Film clubs
And best of all,
Help Others clubs!

 42 Work in small groups. Talk about places you know and what they're known for.

1 Write the names of the places on slips of paper.

2 Write what the places are famous for or known for on other slips of paper.

3 Put the slips into separate bags – one labelled 'Place' and the other labelled 'What It's Known For'.

4 Work with another group. Swap bags.

5 Take turns drawing slips of paper and guessing the place or what it's known for.

6 Continue until all are guessed or revealed.

 Oranges are grown here.

Is it Spain?

43 What are they made of? Use words from the box.

> clay   cotton   metal   rubber   wool

1   Flower pots, plates and floors are made of ❓ .

2   Cola cans and planes are made of ❓ .

3   Tyres and boots are made of ❓ .

4   Warm winter jumpers are made of ❓ .

5   Most T-shirts and sheets are made of ❓ .

 44 Make sentences using the present simple passive form of the verbs.

1   coffee/grow/in Kenya

2   cattle/raise/in Argentina

3   glass beads/make/in Venice

4   cotton/produce/on special farms around the world

45 Make sentences using the past simple passive form of the verbs.

1   the chocolate nut bar/create/Canada

2   the shopping trolley/invent/the United States

3   the first patented karaoke machine/make/the Philippines

4   high speed passenger trains/create/Japan

46 Read and choose.

1   The man **who/where** is coming has a green raincoat.

2   The place **when/where** they went hiking is far from here.

3   The month **when/who** I feel the happiest is December.

4   The dress **which/whose** she chose is really beautiful.

I Can

- **talk about where goods come from.**
- **talk about products and the materials used to make them.**
- **use the passive voice and defining relative clauses.**

HOW ADVENTUROUS ARE YOU?

144

1 Have you ever wondered about the food you eat? Read the fun facts about food. Guess the correct answers. Then listen and check.

1 Refried beans are fried 🦴.

   a twice

   b once

   c three or more times

2 The first soup was probably 🦴.

   a hot vegetable soup

   b cold fruit soup

   c hippopotamus soup

3 The ingredient that makes one popular junk food pop in your mouth is 🦴.

   a just air

   b carbon dioxide

   c sugar

4 Ice cream is actually 🦴.

   a Indian food

   b Italian food

   c Chinese food

5 Blueberries 🦴.

   a may help your memory

   b may help your hearing

   c may cause permanent tooth discolouration

2 Choose two adjectives from the box to describe each food. Then listen and check.

cold	delicious	different	good	hot	popular	pretty	raw
sour	spicy	sweet	tasty	terrible	traditional	unusual	wonderful

Soup from Spain

Soup from China

Japanese Appetiser

Greek Appetiser

Moroccan Dish

Indian Dish

Italian Dessert

Philippine Dessert

3 Point to the foods in 2. Ask and answer with a partner.

Would you rather try the cold soup or the hot soup?

I haven't eaten cold soup before! I'll try it. What's it called?

It's called gazpacho. It's very popular in Spain!

I love it! It's delicious.

THINK BIG What traditional foods do you know? Can you describe their taste? How adventurous are you about food? Is it good to be adventurous about food? Why/Why not?

4 Listen and read. Where is 'ugali' a local food?

HIGH ADVENTURE *at* HIGH ALTITUDES

by Phil Steadman

Explorer Gilda Navarro updates us on her attempt to climb the Seven Summits – the highest mountain on each of the world's seven continents.

Phil Steadman: Good morning, Gilda. Thanks so much for talking to us today. I know you're busy preparing for your next mountain adventure.

Gilda Navarro: Of course, Phil. It's always a pleasure. I could use a break, anyway!

Phil: You certainly have been busy over the last two years.

Gilda: Yes, you could say that!

Phil: For our listeners who may not know, over the last two years you've climbed six of the world's seven tallest mountains. That's amazing for such a short period of time. I get tired just thinking about it!

Gilda: My dad always says I've got a lot of energy.

Phil: That's certainly true! When we last spoke, you were getting ready to climb Mount Kilimanjaro, in Africa. What was it like?

Gilda: That was a great one. Well, they've all been great. Mount Kilimanjaro isn't the highest of the Seven Summits. It's actually number four. It's 5,895 metres high and it's located in Tanzania.

Phil: I see. How long did it take you to climb it?

Gilda: It took me and my team a full seven days to climb that one.

Phil: Wow. What did you eat during the climb? Was it local Tanzanian food?

Gilda: Not really. We had pasta, rice dishes… normal things.

Phil: So the food wasn't as adventurous as the climb, was it?

Gilda: Oh, we had a lot of delicious local food after we got back. There's a tasty Tanzanian food called ugali. Have you ever heard of it?

Phil: No, I haven't. Is it spicy?

Gilda: No, ugali is quite plain by itself. It's made of corn. It looks a little like mashed potatoes. You roll up some ugali in a ball and you dip it in stew.

Phil: That sounds like good comfort food.

Gilda: Yes, I've tried different kinds of food everywhere. I'm pretty adventurous about food, I think.

Phil: What about your next climb?

Gilda: We're getting ready for our last mountain. And we've saved the best for last.

Phil: Mount Everest?

Gilda: That's right. It'll take us a few weeks to climb Everest.

Phil: Is that because it's so high?

Gilda: Well, yes. To climb Mount Everest, you have to stop at several different places and let your body get used to the altitude. If you don't, you'll be in big trouble!

Phil: I bet! I I've got one more question. Imagine you had to choose from one of these: going mountain climbing or going on an all-expenses-paid trip to a gorgeous tropical beach. Which one would you rather do?

Gilda: That's the world's easiest question. I'd rather go mountain climbing! There's nothing better.

Phil: Spoken like a true adventurer! Gilda, thank you for spending time with us. Good luck with that last summit.

Gilda: Thanks so much. It was fun talking to you.

READING COMPREHENSION

5 Read and say true or false.

1 Gilda Navarro has climbed the world's seven highest mountains.

2 Mount Kilimanjaro took Gilda less than a week to climb.

3 Gilda and her group ate local Tanzanian food after their climb.

4 Mount Everest takes weeks to climb to allow time for adjustment to the altitude.

THINK BIG How do you feel about Gilda's attitude to climbing?
Would you ever want to climb a mountain? Why/Why not?
What would you like to ask Gilda about what she has done?

6 Listen and read. Why is Abigail *really* going to go to the concert with her dad?

Dad: Abigail, there's a concert down at the Arts Centre this weekend. Do you want to go?

Abigail: What kind of concert?

Dad: It's classical music. You know… Mozart, Beethoven.

Abigail: Classical music? Uh, no thanks. I'd rather stay at home.

Dad: Come on! Have you ever been to a classical music concert?

Abigail: Well, no… I haven't. But I don't think I'd like it.

Dad: That's a pity because the Arts Centre is giving free BoysTown concert tickets to the first 25 people who come that night.

Abigail: What? The BoysTown concert? I think I've changed my mind.

Dad: Oh, really? Why?

Abigail: Well, Dad, I've never been to a classical music concert before. I might like it. Let's make sure we get there early, OK?

7 Practise the dialogue in 6 with a partner.

8 Listen and match. Then complete the sentences with the correct form of the verb from the box.

> be   learn how   study   try

1 Jason has never ❓ to skateboard.

2 Claire has never ❓ to a water park.

3 Sally has never ❓ Thai food.

4 Allie has never ❓ another language.

Have you ever been to a concert?	Yes, I have./No, I haven't.
Has he ever been skydiving?	Yes, he has./No, he hasn't.

9 Complete the questions. Then make answers.

1 Have you ever ❓ a horror film? (see)

2 Have you ever ❓ skydiving? (be)

3 Have you ever ❓ on a stage? (perform)

4 Have you ever ❓ sushi? (eat)

Would they rather play football or watch it?	They'd rather play football.

10 Look at the survey. Complete the questions. Use would and rather. Then make answers.

1 ❓ play video games or go skateboarding?

2 ❓ write a story or play chess?

3 ❓ visit a museum or create a sculpture?

4 ❓ go fishing or bake a cake?

Pupil Interest Survey

Dear Pupil,
We're putting together an after-school programme and we want
your input! Please tick all activities that interest you. Thanks!

Name: *Chloe Harrison*

- [ ] Baking
- [✓] Sculpture
- [ ] Chess
- [ ] Video game competition
- [✓] Short story writing
- [✓] Fishing
- [✓] Skate-boarding
- [ ] Visiting museums

---

11 Work with your partner. Do these things ever happen to you when you're scared?

1 Your heart beats faster.
2 You feel cold.
3 You feel like you have more energy.
4 You can't concentrate.
5 Your muscles contract.

12 Listen and read. What happens when you're scared?

CONTENT WORDS
adrenal glands adrenalin air cells heart hormone
lungs oxygen prehistoric protect release stress

Fight or Flight

1 Have you ever watched a scary film and felt like your heart was going to jump out of your chest? If so, then you were probably feeling the effects of adrenalin.

2 Adrenalin is an important hormone which is produced by your body. Hormones give important information to different cells. When you get scared, your body sends out adrenalin in order to get itself ready to fight something scary or to run away from it. That's why adrenalin is sometimes called the 'fight or flight' hormone.

3 The release of adrenalin in your body gives you an extra boost of energy. Blood rushes to your muscles so your heart starts beating quickly. Air moves rapidly into your lungs, so you breathe quickly and send oxygen around your body faster. These are normal reactions to fear or stress. What's happening in this situation? This reaction lasts a short period of time. It's just long enough to make you feel stronger and faster and help you deal with a difficult situation. Your body has tried to protect you.

> Adrenalin gets into your cells from your adrenal glands, located at the top of your kidneys.

4 Humans have felt the effects of adrenalin since prehistoric times. Probably the first practical discovery took place when man saw a sabre tooth tiger for the first time! He didn't think, he just ran. However, the official discovery of adrenalin was only made in 1900. But since even before that there have been many stories of people who have used 'superhuman' strength to save another person's life.

5 We feel the effects of adrenalin on a day-to-day basis. In most cases though, the effect is not so dramatic. For example, imagine you're riding on your bike and someone steps out in front of you. Quick! What do you do? Your brain makes a fast decision to get out of the way and the release of adrenalin helps your body move more quickly.

6 So next time you ride a roller coaster, watch a scary film or get nervous before a race, pay attention to how your body reacts. You'll probably be feeling the effects of adrenalin at work.

13 Look at 12. Read and say true or false.

1 Adrenalin is also known as the 'fight or flight' hormone.
2 When adrenalin is released into your body, the heart beats less quickly.
3 'Superhuman' strength is caused by adrenalin in the body.
4 An adrenalin reaction always lasts a very long time.
5 Nobody has discovered how adrenalin works.

14 Use words from 12 to complete the quick facts list.

> **Quick facts about adrenalin**
> • Adrenalin was officially discovered in [1] .
> • Adrenalin is a natural [2] which is released by the [3] in our bodies.
> • The release of adrenalin is our body's reaction to [4] or [5] .
> • Adrenalin makes the [6] beat faster. This pushes more [7] to our muscles and sends more [8] through our lungs and around the body.

15 Work with a partner. Ask and answer. Which activity makes your heart beat fastest? Then order the list (10 is most scary, 1 is least scary).

doing exams		being at home alone	
riding a rollercoaster		sitting in the dark	
riding a bike fast		being very high up	
getting told off at school		being in small spaces	
watching a scary film		seeing spiders or other creepy bugs	

How scary are exams?

I think they're a 5.

Well they aren't very scary but they cause a lot of stress. They make my heart beat really fast.

16 Now compare your answers with another pair. Which activities make you release the most adrenalin? Talk about why.

17 Look, listen and read. What has Harry forgotten to do?

Come on, Harry. I've known you since Primary school. You've wanted to do a bungee jump since you were ten. You've saved all your pocket money for six months. The people in line have waited patiently for almost an hour. Are you going to jump? Or have you changed your mind?

No, no, I haven't. I'm going to jump. I haven't eaten since nine o' clock and I'm really hungry now!

Great, see you at the café when you get down! Bye!

Jennifer! Aaaggh! I've forgotten to take my money out of my pocket!

18 Read and complete.

+	I/You/We/They	¹	**known** each other **since** Primary school.
	He/She/It	²	**saved** his money **for** three weeks.
–	I/You/We/They	**haven't**	**seen** Martin **for** three years.
	He/She/It	**hasn't**	**eaten since** nine o' clock.
?	**Have**	³	**known** Harry **for** a long time?
	⁴	he/she/it	**watched** TV **all** day?
	Yes, I/we/you/they	**have**.	
	Yes, he/she/it	**has**.	
	No, I/you/we/they	**haven't**.	
	No, he/she/it	⁵ .	
How long	⁶	I/you/we/they	**known** that family?
How long	**has**	he/she/it	**been** at the shops?
+	I/You/We/They	**'ve known** them	**since** 2001.
	He/She/It	**'s been** there	**for** three hours.

19 Copy the chart in your notebook. Put the words from the box in the correct column.

> a century   a long time   a month   a year   last night
> Monday   my birthday   twenty days   25ᵗʰ December   2001

For	Since

20 Read and choose.

1   Hande and Batu have been asleep **since/for** four hours.

2   I've played chess **since/for** kindergarten.

3   Our family has had a dog **since/for** last year.

4   Mum's had flu **since/for** a week.

21 Complete using the present perfect and for or since.

1   Carla ❓ a camp leader ❓ five years. (be)

2   Veronica ❓ about bugs ❓ the age of seven. (know)

3   We ❓ tennis ❓ an hour, so we've got more time! (not play)

4   Tara ❓ her grandma ❓ last summer. (not visit)

22 Put the words in order to make questions.

1   lived/has/how long/your/family/in that house/?

2   how long/been/have/you/at your school/?

3   have/known/you/how long/your/best friend/?

4   had/English/lessons/how long/you/have/?

23 Now ask and answer. Answer using for and since. Think of three more How long? questions to ask your partner.

How long has your family lived in that house?

We've lived here for three years. Since 2009.

High Adventure!

We have done extreme activities for centuries. Many of today's extreme sports have their roots in history. Many cultures have encouraged extreme examples of strength or daring. Let's look at some extreme sports.

1 Cliff diving

Competitive divers dive off boards that are between three and ten metres high. But what about diving off the side of a cliff? The La Quebrada Cliff Divers are professional cliff divers. They dive into the sea from a height of 38 metres – head first. There has been a group of professional La Quebrada cliff divers since 1934. However, there are even earlier examples of cliff diving from Lanoii, Hawaii. As early as 1770, local warriors used to throw themselves into the sea to show courage and get the girls!

24 Which extreme sports are popular in your country? Where do people do them? Have you ever tried doing one? Discuss with a partner.

156

25 Listen and read. Why is it called High Adventure?

> **CONTENT WORDS**
> aerialist   antenna   board   competitive diver   extreme sports
> parachute   professional   risk   tightrope   trick   warrior

26 Look at 25. Read and match to paragraphs 1–3.

  a They wanted girls to notice them.

  b In the past, someone used feathers.

  c Someone did it in less than half an hour.

  d They're a talented family.

  e Someone has died doing this.

  f They have had a club for many years.

2 BASE jumping

Have you ever wanted to fly? Stories of tower jumps exist before the flying machine. The earliest recorded jump dates from 852 AD. Arman Firman jumped from a tower in Cordoba, Spain, covered in feathers. BASE jumping is today's tower jumping – only from much higher buildings. BASE jumpers begin by standing at the top of a very high place – BASE stands for Buildings, Antennas, Spans (bridges) and Earth (cliffs). They then take a free jump down, using a small parachute to slow their fall. BASE jumping has been very popular in Norway where you can find the Troll Wall. It's the highest cliff point in Europe – 1,100 metres high. However, since Carl Boennish, the 'father' of BASE jumping, was killed there in 1984, the Norwegian government has banned jumping from it.

3 Tightrope walking

The Frenchman Charles Blondin was the first acrobat to walk a tightrope across Niagara Falls. He crossed the Rainbow Bridge in 1859. Today, the Flying Wallenda Family are aerialists who do tricks high up in the air. In 2012, Nik Wallenda did a 548-metre tightrope walk across the Falls on a tightrope that was only 5 centimetres wide, in only 25 minutes!

Some people love taking extreme risks. Would you try?

27 Work with a partner. Ask and answer about this extreme sport. Complete your fact files.

Student A

Kite Surfing	
Who/invent/it?	?
Where/do it?	On the coast
How long/popular?	?
What/need?	kite, board, wetsuit
How/feel?	?

Student B

Kite Surfing	
Who/invent/it?	Dominique and Bruno Legaignoux from Brittany
Where/do it?	?
How long/popular?	Since the late 1980s
What/need?	?
How/feel?	It's fast and there are jumps and sometimes big waves.

28 Look at 27. Find out about another extreme sport on water and write about it.

THINK BIG Why do you think that some people enjoy extreme sports?

29 Read the paragraph, then copy and complete the chart about it.

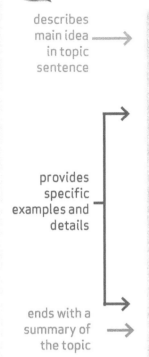

describes
main idea →
in topic
sentence

>   I'm a pretty adventurous person in some ways.
> I love to hike and enjoy hiking on new trails. However,
> I have always been afraid of heights. This is something
> that I'm trying to change about myself because in
> the future I want to hike up a mountain and mountains
> are high! To challenge myself, I've been on the highest rollercoasters
> at the local amusement parks. They were scary but fun! Also, last
> year when I went to Paris, I went on the tour that takes you up to
> the top of the Eiffel Tower. It was a bit scary, too but the view from
> the top was amazing! I may not like heights but I do like adventures.
> And I know one day I'll lose my fear of heights and I'll go and climb that
> mountain!
>
>   – by Stella

provides
specific
examples and
details

ends with a
summary of →
the topic

How Stella is adventurous and willing to try new things – challenges
Example:
Example:

30 Now choose two ways you are adventurous and willing to try new things from the box. Use them to write a descriptive paragraph about yourself.

Challenges
Clothes
Food
Hobbies
Making New Friends
New Places

31 Share your descriptions with the class. Who is the most adventurous?

THINK BIG Is it good to be adventurous? Why/Why not?

32 Answer the questions in your notebook. Then interview a partner and record the answers.

Have you ever... ?	Me		My Partner	
	Yes	No	Yes	No
been to an art show at a local museum				
danced at a local festival or celebration				
helped clean up an area in your community				
seen or talked to the mayor of your town				
volunteered to work with younger children				
visited a local farm				
attended a concert or film at a local park				
had a picnic at a local park				
been swimming at a public beach or pool				
visited someone at a nearby care home				
been to a sports event at another school				
been hiking or camping near where you live				

PROJECT

33 Find photos to make a collage of the things you could explore in your community.

In my community, there are many parks and a lake, too. I've never fished in it but I've been swimming there. I plan to visit a local farm. I've visited a care home and plan to do it again soon!

158

34 Listen, read and repeat.

1 f -t   ft   2 c -t   ct

3 m-p   mp   4 s-k   sk

159

35 Listen and blend the sounds.

1 l-e-f-t   left   2 f-a-c-t   fact

3 c-a-m-p   camp   4 r-i-s-k   risk

5 r-a-f-t   raft   6 l-a-m-p   lamp

160

36 Listen and chant.

> It's a fact that
> Sailing at night
> On a raft,
> Without a lamp,
> Is a risk!

37 Do a survey. On your own, complete each question in your notebook by writing two activities. Then work in groups of four. Take turns asking your questions. Record the answers.

> Would you rather go on a rollercoaster or ride a horse?

> I'd rather ride a horse. Rollercoasters scare me!

Would you rather... ?	Pupil 1	Pupil 2	Pupil 3
go on a rollercoaster or ride a horse			
or			

38 In your group, ask and answer about the activities in your survey.

> Have you ever ridden a horse?

> No, I haven't. But I'd like to try.

39 Complete the sentences with the words from the box. Then answer the questions.

> delicious   spicy   terrible   traditional   unusual

Last night, my family tried a new restaurant in the city. It serves ¹ 🔲 Indian food. My older sister thought the food was too ² 🔲 and started to cough. My brother thought it was so ³ 🔲 that he ordered more. My little sister thought it was ⁴ 🔲 and asked for a cheese sandwich. My Aunt Millie tried a dessert that she'd never had before. She said it was very ⁵ 🔲 but she would order it again.

1   Would her older sister rather eat more or have a glass of water?

2   Would her brother rather not come back or come back often?

3   Would her little sister rather have more Indian food or have something else to eat?

4   Would her aunt rather try another dessert or have the same one again?

40 Answer the questions. Add a sentence that gives additional information.

1   Have you ever eaten Indian food?

2   Have you ever tried a new food and loved it?

3   Have you ever made dinner at home for your family?

4   Have you ever climbed a mountain?

5   Have you ever been on a rollercoaster?

6   Have you ever dived off a cliff?

I Can

• **talk about experiences.**   • **talk about preferences.**

How Well Do I Know It? Can I Use It?

1 Think about it. Read and draw. Practise.

 I know this.   I need more practice.   I don't know this.

	PAGES			
Electronic devices (old and new): transistor radio, video game system, mobile phone…	113	☺	😐	☹
Materials: rubber, wool, cotton…	129	☺	😐	☹
Products: blankets, tyres, T-shirts…	129	☺	😐	☹
Adjectives: delicious, spicy, unusual…	145	☺	😐	☹
What**'s** it **used for?** It**'s used for** reading. What **were** they **used for?** They **were used to** cook.	116–117	☺	😐	☹
It **may** be a mirror. They **might** be ice tongs.	116–117	☺	😐	☹
If I go to bed early, **I don't feel** tired.	120–121	☺	😐	☹
That bracelet **is made** in Switzerland. The first noodles **were** probably **made** in China.	132–133	☺	😐	☹
The man **who** came in is my brother.	136–137	☺	😐	☹
Have you ever **tried** fish? Yes, I **have.**/No, I **haven't.**	148–149	☺	😐	☹
Would you **rather** go hiking or stay at home? I**'d rather** go hiking. I**'d rather not** stay at home.	148–149	☺	😐	☹
I**'ve known** Tom **for** many years. **Since** 2001.	152–153	☺	😐	☹

I Can Do It!

2 Get ready.

A Complete the dialogue using the statements from the box. Then listen and check.

> a I've had it before.
>
> b It's known for its spicy flavours.
>
> c I'd rather try something new tonight.
>
> d I've never had Korean food.
>
> e Some of them are made out of metal.

Dad: Hi, Madeline. What kind of restaurant would you rather go to tonight – Polish or Korean?

Madeline: I don't know. I've tried Polish food but [1] .

Dad: Oh, really? [2] .

Madeline: What's it like?

Dad: It's delicious. [3] . And it usually comes with rice.

Madeline: Sounds interesting. Do you use chopsticks to eat it?

Dad: Yes, a lot of Korean dishes are eaten with both chopsticks and a spoon. But Korean chopsticks are different from other ones.

Madeline: In what way?

Dad: [4] .

Madeline: Really? That's interesting, too.

Dad: So... what do you think – Polish or Korean?

Madeline: [5] . Let's go to the Korean place!

B Practise the dialogue in **A** with a partner.

C Ask and answer the questions with a partner.

1 Have you ever tried Polish food or Korean food?

2 How adventurous are you with new foods? Explain.

3 What's the most unusual food you've ever tried? What was it made of? Would you like to have it again? Why/Why not?

3 Get set.

 STEP 1 Cut out the cards on page 163 of your Activity Book.

 STEP 2 Put the cards facedown and mix them up.
Now you're ready to **Go!**

4 Go!

A Game 1

Work in a small group. Take turns. The first pupil turns over one card. Ask the people in your group.

Have you ever played in a chess tournament?

POINTS:

If no one says *Yes*, keep the card.

If one person says *Yes*, give the card to him/her.

If more than one person says Y*es*, ask: *When*? The person who did it first gets the card.

Continue until the cards are gone.

Try to be the person with the most cards at the end.

B Game 2

First, match each card to the card that has the same beginning word. Then take turns asking questions. When you answer, give a reason.

Would you rather write a short story or an apology email for something you did wrong?

I'd rather write an apology email for something I did wrong. Writing a short story sounds hard to me.

C Tell the class about some of the choices and reasons from your group.

5 Write about yourself in your notebook.

- What's the most adventurous thing you've ever done? Did you enjoy it? Why/Why not?

- Describe an unusual object you've seen before. Where's it from? What's it made of? What's it used for?

All About Me   Date:_____

_____

_____

How Well Do I Know It Now?

6 Look at page 160 and your notebook. Draw again.

A Use a different colour.

B Read and think.

I can ask my teacher for help.

I can practise.

7 Rate this Checkpoint.

 very easy   easy   hard   very hard   fun   OK   not fun

1

2

3

4

5

6

7

8

9

Units 7–9 Exam Preparation

– Part A –

 Listen and write. There is one example.

Example

Where is it?   Opposite the ___rug___ factory

1   Restaurant's address: _____ Park Street

2   Restaurant's name: The _____ Restaurant

3   Food on Tuesdays: Traditional _____ food

4   Times on Sundays: Opens _____ Closes 11:30 p.m.

5   Most unusual food: Sweet and _____ banana cake

Look and read. Choose the correct words and write them on the lines.

Cars have got four of these. They're round.   <u>Wheels</u>

1   This is a hormone that our bodies make
     when we're very scared.   _____

2   We put this on our bed if we're cold.
     It's made of wool.   _____

3   One hundred years make this.   _____

4   Now, we have light bulbs. Before, people used
     these to light their homes.   _____

5   You need this if you jump out of a plane.   _____

6   T-shirts are made of this.   _____

7   You use this when you want to listen to music
     or talk to someone. You don't need to hold it.   _____

8   This comes from a tree. Boots and tyres are made of it.   _____

9   We've got two of these in our body. Air goes into them.   _____

10   We put this in cars to make them run.   _____

Example

a parachute	a century	rubber	towels
lungs	a log	a blanket	cotton
candles	a hands-free earpiece	a heart	
a combustion engine	wheels	adrenalin	

Wordlist

Find these words in your language. Then write them in your notebook.

Unit 1	Page
act	4
analyse	10
art club	6
athletics team	6
basketball team	5
brain	10
build robots	5
competition	7
control	10
creative	10
course	14
determine	10
do martial arts	5
drama club	5
event	14
exchange	10
hemisphere	10
football team	6
instructions	10
jog	5
medals	15
metres	15
motor vehicle	14
Olympic Games	14
paint	6
personality	10
play chess	5
play sports	5
play the trumpet	5
practical	10
race course	14
school newspaper	5
school orchestra	5
school play	7
science club	7
sporting events	14
tae kwon do club	5

take care of	10
variation	14
write articles	9

Unit 2	Page
be born	21
behaviour	26
celebrate	30
decoration	31
find/get a job	25
get married	21
give birth	26
graduate	21
into	30
jaws	26
holiday	28
mammal	26
maternal instinct	26
move	21
offspring	26
open a restaurant	21
powerful	26
predator	26
protect	26
respectively	30
retire	22
ribbon	30
sight	26
sneak	30
special	30
stuff	30
symbolise	30
traditions	30
treat	30
wedding	30
young (n.)	26

Unit 3	Page
advertisement	42
animal rescue	47
animal shelter	46
benefit (v.)	47
bold	42
cancer	46
cause	46
charity groups	46
design posters	37
design	37
donate	46
effective	42
focus	42
font	42
fortune	46
get across	42
have a cake sale	37
have a concert	37
have a dance	38
have an art fair	37
homeless	46
images	42
impatient	42
invisible	42
layout	42
make a video	37
make something	38
post a video/article on the school website	37
proof	46
raise money	37
rescue	46
sell tickets	39
supplies	46
tutoring	46
volunteer	46
write an article	37

Wordlist

Base Form	Past Simple	Base Form	Past Simple	Base Form	Past Simple
ask	asked	help	helped	sing	sang
bake	baked	hit	hit	sit	sat
be	was/were	hold	held	skateboard	skateboarded
begin	began	hope	hoped	sleep	slept
bring	brought	keep	kept	snowboard	snowboarded
build	built	kill	killed	speak	spoke
buy	bought	know	knew	stand	stood
call	called	learn	learnt	start	started
catch	caught	leave	left	stay up	stayed up
celebrate	celebrated	like	liked	swim	swam
change	changed	listen	listened	take	took
come	came	live	lived	talk	talked
cook	cooked	look	looked	tell	told
cut	cut	lose	lost	think	thought
destroy	destroyed	love	loved	throw	threw
do	did	make	made	travel	travelled
draw	drew	meet	met	try	tried
drink	drank	move	moved	turn	turned
drive	drove	need	needed	understand	understood
eat	ate	perform	performed	use	used
explain	explained	plan	planned	visit	visited
fall	fell	play	played	wait	waited
feed	fed	put	put	wake up	woke up
feel	felt	read	read	walk	walked
fight	fought	realise	realised	want	wanted
find	found	rest	rested	wash	washed
fly	flew	ride	rode	watch	watched
get	got	ring	rang	wear	wore
give	gave	run	ran	worry	worried
go	went	say	said	write	wrote
grow	grew	see	saw	yell	yelled
have	had	sell	sold		
hear	heard	send	sent		

Pearson Education Limited
Edinburgh Gate
Harlow
Essex CM20 2JE
England
and Associated Companies throughout the world.

www.pearsonelt.com/bigenglish

© Pearson Education Limited 2015

Authorised adaptation from the United States edition entitled Big English, 1st Edition, by Mario Herrera and Christopher Sol Cruz. Published by Pearson Education Inc. © 2013 by Pearson Education, Inc.

The right of Mario Herrera and Christopher Sol Cruz to be identified as the authors of this Work have been asserted by them in accordance with the Copyright, Designs and Patents Act 1988.

All rights reserved; no part of this publication may be reproduced, stored in a retrieval system, or transmitted in any form or by any means, electronic, mechanical, photocopying, recording, or otherwise without the prior written permission of the Publishers.

First published 2015

ISBN: 978-1-4479-9458-9

Set in Apex Sans
Editorial and design management by hyphen S.A.
Printed in the UK

Acknowledgements

The publisher would like to thank the following for their kind permission to reproduce photographs:

(Key: b-bottom; c-centre; l-left; r-right; t-top)

123RF.com: Aleksandr Kurganov, Audrey Snider-Bell 44t, cycloneproject 98, Elena Elisseeva 66, Melinda Nagy 152b, Mitar Gavric 12b, Mykola Velychko 30l, olegmit1 85br; **Alamy Images:** amana images inc 94t, amana images inc. 157cl, Anatoliy Cherkasov 4-5 (background), 52br, Aurora Photos 84b, B Christopher 51t, Bubbles Photolibrary 75 (c), Creative Control 70, D. Hurst 48t, Dennis MacDonald 85tr, Frankie Angel 113/4, GOIMAGES 113/2, 160 (below centre), Anthony Hatley 47t, Iain Masterton 58br, Image Source 74t, 106t, imagebroker 14l, Janine Wiedel Photolibrary 5/6, Jonah Calinawan 145 (Moroccan), Judy Freilicher 32, Lana Rastro 21/2, Lee-Ann Wylie 155, LOOK Die Bildagentur der Fotografen GmbH 58t, Lynden Pioneer Museum 117bl, MARKA 40, 130tr, MBI 28, mediacolor's 148b, Mira 6b, Myrleen Pearson 47c, 53, 75 (h), 121t, Patti McConville 35b, Peter Phipp / Travelshots.com 69c, redsnapper 82, Simon Price 79, 106 (below centre), Sinibomb Images 41, 113/6, Steve Vidler 68, Stocktrek Images, Inc 96tl, Tetra Images 132l, WENN Ltd 90t, Yulia Kuznetsova 36r; **Corbis:** 68 / Ocean 5/3, DADANG TRI / X01279 / Reuters 136c, Google / Handout 90bl, KHAM / Reuters 136l; **DK Images:** Dave King,Steve Gorton,Andy Craw 126/3, Karen Trist 117br, Robert Schweizer 85tl, Susanna Price 24; **Fotolia.com:** 2tun 59 (bracelet), Aaron Amat 126/4, Adrian 131l, Africa Studio 59 (balloons), alarsonphoto 59 (earrings), 106 (above centre), alessandrozocc 118/2, andersphoto 134 (lettuce), Andrey Kuzmin 134 (knife & fork), Anibal Trejo 142t, arinahabich 156, arquiplay77 129/3, Arto 4cr, Artur Synenko 64c, asese 10b, 52 (above centre), AVAVA 105, Barbara Helgason 59 (frame), Beatrice Kesseler 140, beatrice prève 6t, biker3 103, bkhphoto 87c, bondsza 4br, BVDC 21/4, 52t, Canadeez 90br (dog), chris2766 125tl, Chrispo 138tl, Claudio Divizia 64bl, 106bl, Cybrain 128tr, Darrin Henry 46, Denis Pepin 38, Denys Prykhodov 90br (mobile), dja65 126/1, DM7 102, donatas1205 113/1, Douglas Knight 14r, 52bl, duckman76 4tr, EJ White 15b, 17r, 27cr, 37bl, 99r, 113br, 119l, 121br, 137r, 142br, 157 (boy), Elenathewise 138tr, emese73 10t, 153t, EpicStockMedia 74 (background), eurobanks 128c, exclusive-design 144-145 (background), Fotokon 64t, Frédéric COIGNOT 131r, Gelpi 5bl, 11l, 29l, 45r, 48br, 59bl, 69br, 81l, 83bl, 91bl, 119r, 127l, 129br, 135r, germanskydive110 149t, GoodMood Photo 129/1, gwimages 15c, Haslam Photography 59 (roses), Herjua 20t, higyou 96b, hitdelight 138b, 139t, Igor Klimov 91 (b), 106bc, iofoto 78t, Jacek Chabraszewski 36l, JJAVA 144t, 145 (Indian), 160t, Joe Gough 159, JonMilnes 112/3, Julián Rovagnati 149b, Kadmy 35/1, kaphotokevm1 35/4, KaYann 130tl, Ken Hurst 9bl, 17l, 21bl, 27tl, 151l, 158br, Kzenon 20br, Lisa F. Young 25, 37/2, littleny 20bl, mast3r 37/3, MasterLu 130br, Meliha Gojak 139b, Michael Flippo 71, micromonkey 15t, milachka 9t, Milos Tasic 129/2, 160 (above centre), mirabella 59 (necklace), Mitchell Knapton 75 (g), Monkey Business 5/2, 8, 75 (a), 157l, Natalia Danecker 144 (below centre), Nathan Allred 21/3, Oleksiy Mark 128b, 160bl, Olesia Bilkei 129/4, paylessimages 123tr, percent 129/5, petunyia 75 (d),

plutofrosti 91 (d), robert lerich 145 (Greek), romikmk 144 (above centre), Sergey Novikov 141b, sframe 143, Simone van den Berg 36c, skynet 133, soundsnaps 113/3, strelov 126/2, sumnersgraphicsinc 128tl, tarei 26tr, Tombaky 39, tr3gi 118/1, Tupungato 141t, Ulrich Müller 134 (background), volgariver 130bl, Wang Hsiu-Hus 80bl, WINIKI 122, zagorskid 90c; **Getty Images:** AFP / Yoshikazu Tsuno 112/1, Ben Speck & Karin Ananiassen 101l, Creative / Uwe Umstatter 116 (boy & girl), Imagemore Co, Ltd. 152t, The Image Bank / Terence Langendoen 75 (f); **Glow Images:** Blend RF 20c, Bridge / Jim Cummins 5/4, Caroline Mowry / Somos Images / Corbis 118/5, Henry Georgi / Aurora Open 74b, ImageBroker / Ulrich Doering 5/1, Laureen Morgane / Corbis 74c, 87t, Newscom / JP5 / ZOB / WENN.com 112/2, NordicPhotos 37/1, PhotoNonStop / Eurasia Press 69t, Purestock 33b, Uppercut 21/1; **Newscom:** Jaime Avalos / EFE 101r, Lin Bin / Xinhua / Photoshot 100, Splash News / Opulent Items 123tl; **Pearson Education Ltd:** Jon Barlow 27br, 37br, 47bl, 72l, 91bc (left), 99l, 113bl, 121bl, 137l, 142bl, 145bl, 153bl, Gareth Boden 59br, 72r, 81r, 125br, 129bl, 132r, 135l, 151l, 158tl, Sozaijiten 83t; **Photo Researchers, Inc.:** Dante Fenolio / Science Source 26tl; **PhotoEdit Inc.:** Jeff Greenberg 51b; **Photoshot Holdings Limited:** C. C. Lockwood 26b; **Rex Features:** MOBA 84t; **Shutterstock.com:** 3Dstock 91 (a), 95b, Andresr 33t, Antonio V. Oquias 145 (Philippine), AVAVA 91br, baitong333 80tl, bonchan 145 (Spain), C Salisbury 60 (camouflage), Carlos Caetano 19, charles taylor 16, Cherkas 60b, Daniel Padavona 145 (Italian), Danny Smythe 88, Dmitry Kolmakov 136r, Elena Elisseeva 80 (background), Elena Schweitzer 58-59 (background), Elzbieta Sekowska 157r, 160br, ESTUDI M6 154, eurobanks 5br, 9br, 11r, 21br, 27tr, 29r, 45l, 47br, 48bl, 69bl, 83br, 85bl, 91bc (right), 127r, 158tr, 158bl, Feng Yu 123 (bag), Fernando Blanco Calzada 91 (c), fet 5/5, fotohunter, Graeme Shannon 27bl, HomeStudio 116 (abacus), ifong 144-145b, Ivonne Wierink 42, 52 (below centre), Jacek Chabraszewski 58bl, 106br, Jaimie Duplass 12t, Jason Winter 113 (background), Jeff Banke 80br, JHDT Stock Images LLC 145br, 153br, Karkas 67, Looper 21 (banner), marekuliasz 61, marylooo 30 (background), MaszaS 75 (e), MaxyM 157cr, Melanie DeFazio 35/3, Michael J Thompson 124, Michelle Eadie 146-147 (background), Mike H 94b, Mikhail Zahranichny 75 (i), Monkey Business Images 148t, Nata-Lia 60t, Natali Glado 63, Ociacia 96tr, Oleksandr Chub 113/5, Patrick Breig 95t, Peter Zvonar 118/3, photosync 123b, Poznukhov Yuriy 44b, quetton 84 (background), Renata Sedmakova 125tr, Robert Kneschke 35/2, rprongjai 145 (Japanese), Rudy Balasko 118/4, Sebastian Kaulitzki 150, Sharon Day 117t, Shutterstock.comPhotographer / CHQualifier 145 (China), Susan Leggett 75 (b), Tom Hirtreiter 87b, Tomasz Trojanowski 62, vrvalerian 122-123 (background), XiXinXing 31, Ysbrand Cosijn 30r; **SuperStock:** Exactostock 78b

Cover images: *Front:* **Shutterstock.com:** Charlie Hutton l, Elzbieta Sekowska c; **SuperStock:** Fancy Collection r

All other images © Pearson Education

Every effort has been made to trace the copyright holders and we apologise in advance for any unintentional omissions. We would be pleased to insert the appropriate acknowledgement in any subsequent edition of this publication.

Illustrated by

Paula Franco, Carl Pearce, Anthony Lewis, Zaharias Papadopoulos (hyphen), Jessica Secheret, Christos Skaltsas (hyphen)